Dynamics of Banjo Sound

by Tom Nechville

1 2 3 4 5 6 7 8 9 0

© 2012 BY MEL BAY PUBLICATIONS, INC., PACIFIC, MO 63069.
ALL RIGHTS RESERVED. INTERNATIONAL COPYRIGHT SECURED. B.M.I. MADE AND PRINTED IN U.S.A.
No part of this publication may be reproduced in whole or in part, or stored in a retrieval system, or transmitted in any form
or by any means, electronic, mechanical, photocopy, recording, or otherwise, without written permission of the publisher.

Visit us on the Web at www.melbay.com — E-mail us at email@melbay.com

Table of Contents

Introduction 3

Chapter One—Evaluating a Banjo 6
    First Impression 6
    Appearance 6
    Feel 6
    Weight 7
    Balance 8
    Sound 8
    Playability 8

Chapter Two—How Banjos Work 9
    Unwanted Non-Musical Resonance 10
    Tone Ring and Rim Combination 10
    Neck Woods 11
    The Bridge 12
    Break Angle 13

Chapter Three—Warming Up Your Banjo 14
    Heads 14
    Bridges 15
    Bridge Weight 15
    String Slots 15
    Bridge Height 15
    Tailpieces 16
    Summary 16

Chapter Four—Heading for Great Sound 17
    Remo Heads 17
    5-Star Heads 18
    Heading My Way 18
    Head Tightening 18
    Heading for Tradition 20
    Heading for Expression 21
    Electric Heads? 21

Chapter Five—"Magic" Bridges 22
    Musicality 23
    Sustain 23
    Chimes and Bell-like Tone 24
    Bass Response 24
    Wide Sound 24

Chapter Six—Tailpiece Adjustments 25
    Types of Tailpieces 26

Chapter Seven—Tone Rings 27
    Aluminum-Bodied Banjos 27
    Old-time Tone Rings 27
    Spun Tone Rings 28
    The Mastertone Rings 28
    Archtop Tone Rings 28
    Flat Head Tone Rings 28
    Problems with Tone Rings 29
    Cyclotronic and Timbre-Tronic Tone Rings 30

Chapter Eight—Don't Crank Those Rods! 32
    The Flux Capacitor 33

Chapter Nine—Fine Tuning Your Neck (and Other Intonation Secrets) 34
    Bridge Placement 34
    Neck Bow and Truss Rod Adjustment 35
    Fine-Tuning the Nut 35
    Touch Up the Frets 36

Chapter Ten—Step-by-Step to Professional Banjo Set-Up 37

Chapter Eleven—How to Play the Banjo 39

Appendix—Notes from the Author 41

About the Author 43

Nech-tology 101, A Glossary of Nechville Terms 44

Introduction

    As a guy who has spent more time than most on the subject of getting banjos to sound good, I'm glad to finally get the opportunity to pass along what I have learned about the banjo. I won't go deeply into the physics of sound or be sidetracked by too many theoretical hunches, but I'll try to stick to facts as much as possible. My favorite instrument is interesting to work on and rewarding to play. I live every day in anticipation of the musical payoff when my banjo is tuned up and making just the right sounds. Then, I can finally let loose and really enjoy just playing. Alone or with people, the banjo has the capacity to transport your thoughts and emotions to new places.

    Thank you for your desire to learn about the workings of America's beloved instrument. As one who has lived for decades in and around people with the same banjo obsession, I realize for the purposes of reaching a wider audience, it is important to step back and begin this book with the novice or layman in mind. Whether you are a player, repairman, or just curious about this interesting instrument, I hope you'll benefit from this comprehensive study of the inner workings of the banjo.

    The banjo can be classified into 2 main headings: 4-string and 5-string. Certainly there are also 1, 2, 3, 6, 7, 8, 10 and 12 string banjos in the world, but 4 and 5-string banjos define our subject for this book.

    Tenor and plectrum 4-string banjos are used in Dixieland jazz, old American show tunes, and Irish and Celtic music. The 4 strings of a plectrum banjo can be easily tuned to the first 4 strings of a guitar. The term "plectrum" refers to the method of playing it, with a plastic flat pick. Guitarists tend to grab the plectrum banjo when the sound of a banjo is called for because of the easy transition from guitar. Tenor banjos could also be considered "plectrum" banjos because they are also played with a plectrum (or flat pick), but we only call the long-neck 4 strings "plectrums ." Tenor banjos are usually tuned with each successive string five whole musical steps above the next lower string. This tuning in "5ths" is similar to mandolin or violin tuning, so the tenor is popular for multi-instrumentalists. The tenor is especially welcome in Irish traditional band configurations. This tuning makes for full-sounding chords, and gives the tenor a wide range of notes.

As a 5-string player all my life, it is surprising how few 4-string players I encounter in my banjo travels. It's not that 4-string banjos are rare, but it seems to be that 4 stringers and 5 stringers tend to live in separate worlds. There is very little crossover musically, or opportunity to meet with 4-string players when you are a bluegrass guy. Plectrum and tenor players do hang out together, but I'm not sure what would happen if a 5-string player showed up at a 4-string banjo gathering. I imagine they would politely welcome you to play along and then blow you away with their plectrum-induced volume.

The cultures are entirely different. Showing up with a plectrum style banjo at a bluegrass jam might be considered even more out of place. I think this unfortunate division is a little bit "un-American." In the spirit of patriotic unity and brotherly love, the diverse worlds of 4 and 5-string banjos ought to converge as a model for the rest of the world. So what if we have different religions, different tastes, different ages, different customs? Let's start being inclusive and we'll discover that we have more in common than we ever thought we did.

Bluegrass dominates 5-string banjo playing. However, 5-string banjos can also be divided into two main categories: those with resonator back covers called bluegrass banjos and those without resonators called open back or old-time banjos. Bluegrass banjo is finger picked with two metal finger picks and a plastic thumb pick. Old-time banjo is frailed with a bare finger downstroke followed by a percussive strum and thumb stroke. Quick double-thumbing and intricate left hand hammers and pull-offs give the old-time player a versatility that enables the clawhammer player to even pull off complex fiddle melodies. Of the 5-string banjo music being produced today, I would say that bluegrass style 3-finger playing has remained the most dominant, although there seems to be growing popularity in frailing or "clawhammer" playing as heard in old-time and mountain music. Countless string bands of the younger generations have had success with the folky sounds of 5-string open back banjos.

While hard-core old-timey groups may at first seem exclusive and alienating to bluegrassers, the worlds of bluegrass and old-time are peacefully co-existing. These groups are beginning to converge more, thanks to bluegrass and old-time festival and event organizers who are cognizant of the need to honor the old traditions while celebrating the newest and most innovative music the world has seen. Organizations such as IBMA, (International Bluegrass Music Association) encourages the commercialization of bluegrass and old-time, (as well as related acoustic music outside of bluegrass) while honoring the pioneers of the music and preserving the traditional flavor and wholesome attitude of America's folk music. Without such organizations that bring together all styles of music played with primarily acoustic (not electric) instruments, a new rift might develop, potentially segregating devotees of old versus those of the new. Therefore, social groupings of like-minded musicians has its parallel to ethnic groupings of people around the world. Segregation may lead to misunderstanding, prejudice, discrimination, and worse. I'm not saying that the solution to all our world's problems is as easy as inviting all nations to a giant bluegrass festival, but it might be.

Late 19th and early 20th century parlour music featured 5-string banjo classically fingerpicked by virtuoso musicians. The fad eventually faded but the banjo re-emerged in the hands of bluegrass style finger pickers of early country music. The banjo was popularized by a series of pioneering players throughout the 20th century. I consider Earl Scruggs, Don Reno, and Bill Keith as the main pioneers who led to today's bluegrass and newgrass picking. Of course, Earl was the master who devised a pattern-oriented finger roll technique for the 5-string which still dominates bluegrass. Don Reno combined more of a guitar approach to melody with the 3 finger method, by employing his thumb and index finger alternately as if he was using an up and down flat pick motion. This technique enabled the mastery of scale-oriented single note melodies to be played in conjunction with Scruggs rolls. Bill Keith, and also Bobby Thompson, added to the mix the ability to play scale melodies by using particular left-hand fingerings that enabled scale segments to be played with simple Scruggs-like rolls. Contemporary 3 finger artist, Tony Trischka, and his protégé Bela Fleck, have seamlessly integrated Scruggs' roll patterns, Reno's single-string method, and Keith/Thompson melodic style, bringing 3-finger picking to heights unimagined a few decades ago.

The purpose here is not to detail banjo history, but to provide a backdrop to view the banjo as what it is, a vibrant, growing and evolving musical instrument. The banjo has received more than its share of punishment for being associated with white "minstrel shows" and entertainment at the expense of African-Americans. The chapter in history that featured the banjo in mockery of another "class" is long over. Despite the faint lingering impression that the banjo was somehow complacent with racial injustice, the banjo survives, and is in fact flourishing in today's society which demands "political correctness." Although our country's history also has dark spots, the banjo continues to offer illumination and hope for what is best about our great land.

Having established a respect for this uniquely American instrument, we have a good foundation for seeing what can be done to improve the state of our beloved banjo. Please feel free to visit our web site, www.nechville.com, for a look at the very latest in banjo technology and design improvements.

Chapter One
Evaluating a Banjo

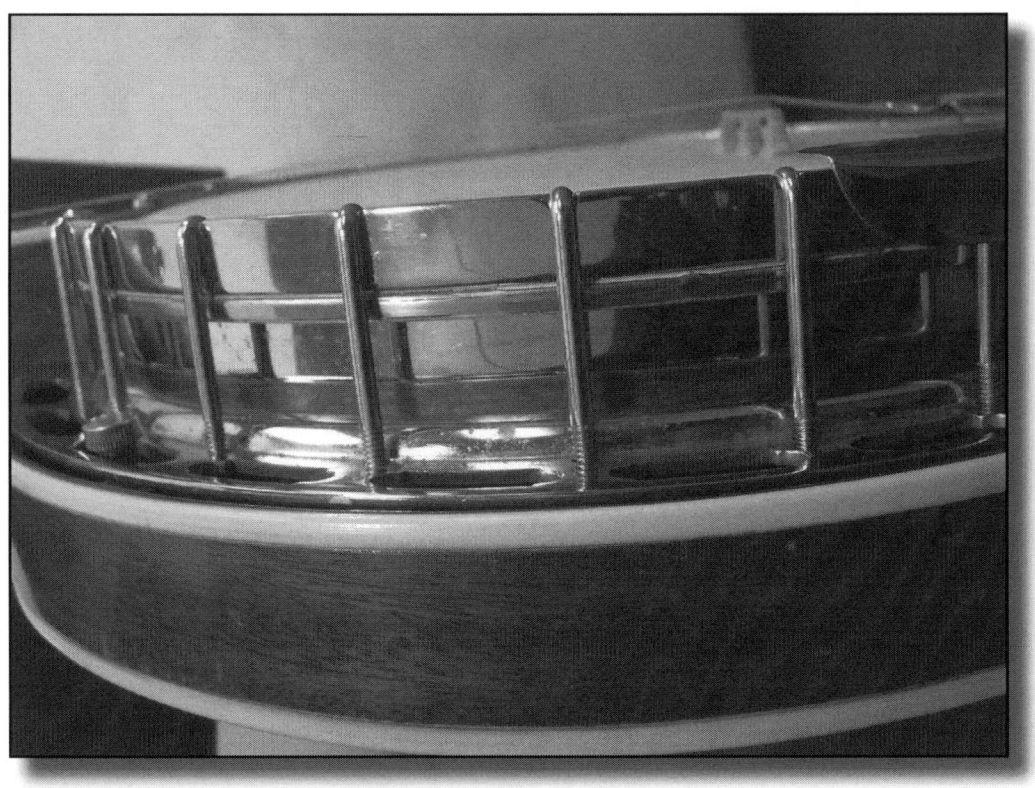

Assuming you already have a banjo, you'll first need to evaluate the quality of the instrument and diagnose any problem that it may have. Much of what I have to say here also applies when you are considering buying a banjo.

First Impression
When you pick up a banjo, what is the first thought that pops into your head? Are you inspired to play by the mere feel and look of it? What about the sound? If it's an expensive banjo, there's a better chance that it has been well set-up by the maker or other luthier. Your banjo should draw you in to want to play it. It need not be an expensive instrument to have this quality, but it will likely require a bit more effort to produce that inspirational "play-me" allure if it is your typical garage sale special. Let's evaluate several aspects of your banjo, starting with its appearance, feel, weight, balance, sound and playability.

Appearance
Is your banjo shiny and new or rusty and old? Does the instrument have any eye-catching elements that are unique? Visual character contributes to the inspirational quality of your banjo. If it's dusty and dirty, take some time to polish it up. Use some 409 cleaner on the head, or use a pencil eraser to get the marks off. Take some 0000 steel wool to polish the frets. Use some "mirror glaze" or similar polish to buff out the scratches.

Feel
When you grab the neck of your instrument, you should take note of the thickness and width of the neck. Slim, low-profile necks are a little easier to play and feel better in the hand. It is possible to re-shape chunky necks by sanding them down to size and then refinishing them. But this kind of work is drastic and usually not a practical option. If you are curious what desirable dimensions would be, I offer the following dimensions used in Nechville

necks: Thickness from the top of the fingerboard surface (not including a fret itself) to the back side of the neck at the 1st fret is .78". Width at the first fret is about 1 1/4". Thickness at the 12th fret is about .84", and the width there is about 1 3/4".

Another critical aspect of feel is having smooth fret ends. Do you feel the sharp edges of the frets sticking out the side of the fingerboard? That happens if a neck is made during high humidity conditions but dries out during dry winter months. You can use a fine flat file or flat diamond stone used for sharpening knives to bevel the ends of the frets so they feel comfortable to the hands. Hold the file lengthwise at a 45-degree angle and use careful firm strokes until the file barely touches the top corner of the fingerboard. Of course the methods suggested in this book require a steady hand and some skill with tools to avoid scratches and dings. So if you lack confidence with any of my suggestions, seek help from us or another qualified luthier.

To enhance the feel even more, you can round the corners of each fret end with a small file or emery board. If you work on fretted instruments as a hobby or professionally it may be worthwhile to acquire or make special tools for this purpose. I like to use a small file that has had the corners dulled so as to avoid gouges adjacent to the frets. Finish up by polishing the frets with some 400 to 1000 grit sandpaper. You may use ultra fine (0000) steel wool with a few drops of lemon oil right over the frets and finger board to clean and rejuvenate the appearance and feel of the fret board. Afterwards you can wipe the neck clean with a dry cloth. Perfectly level frets are a critical part of good sound and playability so please see additional tips in *Chapter IX*.

Another feel factor is how your right arm contacts the banjo body or pot. Usually there is a metal armrest in place that buffers the sharp edge of the banjo's top tension hoop and prevents your right arm from dampening the vibrating head. Many armrests can still be irritating to the forearm, restricting circulation—sometimes to the point of numbness, especially after extended play. Nechville has developed a replacement beveled wooden armrest adaptable to most banjos which allows for more comfortable play without the constant stress of a hard metal edge against the arm. See www.nechville.com for availability information.

Weight

While weight is often a sign of good quality in banjos, heaviness can also present problems especially taking its toll on the shoulders and back over long periods of play. Solidly-built and tightly-assembled instruments need not be overly heavy to produce a bright and lovely sound but the majority of professional bluegrass banjos have a heavy-duty body made of a thick wooden rim capped with a dense metal tone ring which the head is stretched over. Heavy weight is your first clue about the sound potential of the instrument. If set up properly this type of banjo can produce the brilliance and volume often preferred by bluegrassers. If you are like me and play a lot standing up, you'd appreciate the lightest weight possible without sacrificing great, inspiring tone. With a wider range of tone rings available from Nechville and others, players today can choose lighter combinations of tone components without sacrificing any quality of sound. Old-time or mountain style clawhammer players are almost united in their preference for lighter weight banjo rims as the accepted standard for their genre.

Nechville's Comfort Bevel Armrest

Balance

Another important factor to consider when evaluating your instrument is how it balances in your lap and how it hangs from the strap that you may be using. If the peghead falls down and you must expend energy just to hold the neck up, your left arm will quickly tire, leading to curtailed practice sessions. In order to get the most out of your practice, you should spend as much time as possible at each sitting. Invest in a good strap and take the time to adjust it so the neck remains at a comfortable playing angle unaided.

Sound

Beginners need only a clear note and easy playability through the early stages of learning. The benefit of high quality can not be overstated, however. Good musical tone and easy playability will vastly facilitate the speed of your learning and make the process more enjoyable. A simple brush over the tuned strings is enough to tell if the tone will be acceptable to you. Since banjo bridges can be moved around on the head of the banjo, it is very common for banjo bridges to be misplaced, therefore causing poorer pitch intonation the further you fret the strings up the neck. While the fine positioning of the bridge is covered in detail later in this book, it will suffice for now to understand that the 12th fret should be the halfway point to the bridge.

Use a long ruler or tape measure to make sure the bridge is the same distance from the 12th fret as the 12th fret is to the zero fret, or "nut" as it is called. Great sound has an intoxicating effect upon the player, and if played well, also upon the listener. The purpose of this book is to educate every player about the design of the instrument so that he or she will understand the instrument entirely, therefore being able to make the appropriate adjustments or changes that lead to optimal and inspiring tone.

If you are facing a problem with an unwanted buzzing sound, the problem can always be corrected either through securing a loose component, or more commonly, through correcting the cause of fret buzzing. The cause of fret buzz is either overly low action, or an overly high level of one or more frets. A higher bridge is often a quick fix, while leveling the frets requires a little more investment of time or money. If you are facing a dull, lifeless tone, perhaps the strings are too old, the head is too loose, and/or the bridge is mismatched to the banjo. All of these modifications are covered in detail later in the book.

Playability

Much of this book is devoted to the issue of playability. What this entails is having the strings close to the frets so they are easy to press down and the banjo plays in tune. This distance from the top of the 12th fret to the bottom of the 3rd string is called the "string action" of your instrument. Ideal action should be under 1/8". As you know, if action is too low, strings will buzz on the frets, making the instrument unplayable. Low action, however, is much better than high action because it is easy to fix low action. High action is cause for serious concern and is a major reason for seeking out a better banjo. Much will be said in following chapters about the importance of the bridge upon sound and playability. Bridge height on each string is important for ease of play in combination with perfect sound. Don't worry, we'll get there. Just remember that if strings are too low to the frets, the problem is generally easy to fix, but not so if strings are already too high and the bridge is 5/8" or lower.

Chapter Two
How Banjos Work

    The purpose of this chapter is to give you an overview of how the components of traditional and modern banjos work together to produce musical sound.

    Stated simply, a banjo is a drum on a stick! Rather than a resonant wooden box for a sound chamber as in a guitar, the banjo's sound chamber is a heavily constructed drum. The light flexible drum head, when stretched tight, efficiently transfers the vibrating string energy into vibrating diaphragm energy, much like a speaker in your stereo. The sound of a banjo is unmistakably bright because of this direct transfer of string energy into the head, which is tight with potential energy.

    The various nuances of tone that banjos make depend upon the many adjustments discussed in this book. The main distinguishing characteristic of a banjo is its head and the discussion of how much tension it should have, and the best method for tightening it, are central issues here. There are only two main methods of tightening the head on a banjo. The traditional tensioning mechanism is comprised of a series of threaded hooks, or bolts, around the perimeter of the head. Each hook has a nut which needs to be equally tight. If adjustable bolt heads are exposed and adjustable from around the top perimeter of the head, it's called a "top-tension" banjo. Both "hook and nut" and top-tension banjos act to pull a stiff hoop, called the tension hoop, down to pull the head tight. Although there are many parts to tighten evenly, the traditional drum hoop design is simple, economical, and effective.

    The alternate style of head tension, introduced to the world of bluegrass during the decade of the 1990's, is known as helical head mounting. Nechville, the inventor and patent holder of helical head mounting, continues to make the new design accessible to more players each year. Differing dramatically from the traditional design, the drum body or "pot" comprised of the tone ring and rim is mounted concentrically into a metal frame called a Heli-Mount, which is fastened to the neck. There is a singular screw thread around the inside perimeter of the Heli-mount frame that acts like the threaded ridges around the lip of a jar. A threaded mating retaining ring is turned into the back of the frame, securing and tightening the tone ring, or rim body against the head.

The function of any banjo depends on the efficient transfer of energy from your picking motion into string vibrations. The string vibrations in turn must efficiently transmit into head vibrations via the bridge, which in turn activates the air into sound waves. The active transducing elements that work together to create the banjo's sound are the strings, bridge, and head. These are the most active vibrating components, but obviously the structure that the head is stretched upon is also important in defining the quality of the banjo's sound. At this point, let us assume that the string gauges, bridge specifications, head type, and head tension are all functioning optimally, and let's look at the rest of the instrument and how various components can affect your overall sound.

First, there are two sides to the head, each side producing sound waves emanating in two directions. Assume first that the strings are anchored rigidly, and that the head's perimeter is immovably fixed upon a solid base. There would be an equal amount of sound projection going in both directions, in front of the banjo and inside the banjo. There isn't much we can do with the sound that leaves the head and travels out directly toward the listener's ear, unless we consider the combined effect of this sound with the other half of the sound that is processed through the tone chamber of the banjo's pot or body. The portion of sound energy passing through the inside of the banjo becomes "processed" by the interior geometry of the banjo's body.

The inside of the banjo can be compared to a type of megaphone—its function being to funnel the sound out the back, or if the banjo has a resonator, turn the sound around and direct it forward toward the listener. Resonators reflect most of banjo's sound forward, losing a bit of the vibrational energy to the wood, but emanating a portion of the sound from the sound ports around its perimeter. The combined sound of the front and back of the head lends a bit of natural reverberation to the banjo sound, having half of the sound traveling a bit further to reach the listener's ear, thereby creating the acoustic resonator effect.

All banjos function with these basic principles, but factors that create differences in tone quality are much more complicated. Not being a scholar in the physics of sound, I tread on thin ice with some of my theories, but I am confident that most of my observations can be confirmed as true.

To recap, vibrations from the picked strings cause slight pressure variations on the surface of the banjo head, resulting in sound. As mentioned, there are other indirect vibrational effects occurring simultaneously to color the tone. Vibrations also pass directly from the head to the pot via direct contact of touching parts. All parts are connected so they will all resonate with their own "voice." Another vibrational effect is the way that airborne sound waves affect the materials inside a banjo. Sound not only reflects off the resonator, but is colored by the wood's own natural resonance. Luthiers hope that their work will help enhance a warm or woody nuance in an instrument. A common problem however, in a hook and nut banjo, is its tendency to transfer vibrations to all of the banjo's hardware with unpredictable results.

Unwanted Non-Musical Resonance

As stated previously, all parts of the banjo are connected together, so even if you have taken great care to select the most desirable and beautiful-sounding musical woods, the overall sound of your banjo tone will be greatly influenced by the attachment of all of the banjo's metal parts. To varying degrees, a metallic nuance that I sometimes call a "ragged edge" is present in most banjos. While your ears may be accustomed to the typical metallic banjo brightness, some listeners may key in on a quality that seems overly harsh or shrill. If you suspect your instrument is picking up too much of the metallic edge, read on, as there are several things you can try in order to smooth out the tone.

Tone Ring and Rim Combination

The materials that the body of your banjo is made from affect its acoustic properties. As mentioned earlier, heavy, well-fit components of tone ring and rim often form the foundation of a good banjo body. This combination generally lends to a solid and bright tone. The "standard" tone ring material (in bluegrass and many 4-string banjos) is some variation of bell bronze. The tone ring itself weighs a bit over 3 pounds. Ideally, it fits easily on the wooden rim without forcing and without rattling. The preferred rim is made from three plies of rolled hard maple, and its quality depends upon its lack of soft spots, or voids, in the wood, plus a good intimate fit to the tone ring.

A tall wooden rim by itself, shaped to replace both the tone ring and the rim produces a less powerful sound than the heavy bluegrass banjo pot, but usually has a pleasant "woody" tone.

As a general rule, harder and dense materials in the tone ring/rim (or "pot") cause a brighter, louder sound. A dense, heavy pot—without sound-absorbing voids or soft spots between the rim and tone ring—will provide a great "inertia base" for the head to be stretched upon. In other words, the heavy pot won't yield to or absorb vibrations from the head, and the head will vibrate longer (producing sustain) and with more amplitude (volume).

Old-time banjo pots tend to be thinner and more absorbing of the head's vibrations, although they often impart a pleasant quality to the banjo's tone. The only problem with the heaviest, most dense, and best-fitting tone ring and rim in the world is that it masks nothing. The resulting sound might be loud and ringing, but such a naked, unmasked banjo sound in a conventional banjo can be too harsh or bright for some musical situations.

One reason I think that old tone rings from the 1930s are sought-after is that they contain a relatively large amount of softer trace elements in the metal recipe. Pure bell bronze is copper and tin only, but this formula has not gained as much favor, presumably due to its ringy quality that supports high frequency sounds. Banjos with this formula ring can be found that sound wonderful, but some may consider the tone to be too bright. The pre-war tone rings that have been tested and analyzed have been found to contain zinc, lead, magnesium, and other trace metals.

It remains a point of controversy, but my opinion is that it was common for early banjo makers to employ brass foundries that also made general-purpose castings for plumbing fixtures and industrial parts. It is therefore likely that the banjo tone rings of the day were made from general purpose bronze that was common in plumbing fixtures or industrial parts. This may be why it's hard to find two old tone rings made from the exact same formula.

Today most tone rings are still made from copper alloys containing several elements, including zinc and lead. These materials tend to deaden the tone ring from excess ringiness, but generally retain the inertia mass of the heavy pot structure. The notion that the tone ring holds all the secrets to a great banjo sound is overstated, however. If the only difference between 2 banjos was a change in metallurgy of the tone ring, you would have a hard time detecting any difference between the different instruments.

For a look at more types of tone rings, consult *Chapter VII* on tone rings.

Neck Woods

When considering the effect of a neck upon the sound, it is helpful to remember that the strings have two attachment points. At each end of the strings, the character of the string's vibrations will be colored by the solidity of the string's two attachment points. Having the strings anchored to the neck at the peghead, the neck reacts to the vibrating string with a corresponding vibration of its own. As foreshadowed in the previous tone ring example, the rigid and dense components yield less to the energy supplied from the vibrating string. For example, a strong neck made of hard maple allows a greater amount of energy to be transferred to the strings, resulting in more sustain or potential for brilliance.

Maple is perhaps the most common banjo wood because of its relative strength and rigidity. The stiffer quality of maple results in a neck with a bit less tendency for absorption of string vibrations. The resulting sound is bright with good sustain. The same reasoning applies to the banjo's fingerboard material. Ebony is harder and denser than rosewood, so one would expect a bit more warmth from the rosewood and more brightness from the ebony. If an entire neck was made from ebony, there would likely be very good sustain, but perhaps a lack of some warmth.

Mahogany is a softer wood than maple, but it is very stable. Honduras mahogany is a good choice for banjo necks because it changes little with weather and humidity variations. It also reacts with the string to allow most of the volume, but facilitates a nice balance of tonal characteristics. The mahogany sound is a bit more "honey-like" and smooth, but does not drop off in sustain as much as you would imagine for a softer wood.

Walnut is a good compromise between maple and mahogany because its hardness usually falls in between the two. It has a warm, bassy tone and a nice balance. Curly walnut tends to be the warmest and "driest" of the three woods discussed, which results in a bit less sustain. Watch out for "burly walnut" for necks. While the grain may look cool, it can be unstable dimensionally. The mass and size of the neck factors in here as well. It is common to add a bit more mass when using softer woods such as walnut and mahogany for a neck.

The Bridge

The banjo bridge is one part of a banjo that, if changed or adjusted only slightly, may yield dramatic changes in tonal characteristics. Since the sound-producing string energy is transmitted via the bridge, you can imagine that the bridge would be a critical component of the banjo system. The mass of a bridge can be too high, leading to a muffled or quiet and sustaining sound, or it can be too light, and sound wimpy, too brittle or harsh. The exact weight bridge for your banjo depends on several factors, including how the rest of the banjo is set up and what your personal preferences in tone are.

Most professionals prefer a little warmer tone—so a little extra bridge mass becomes important. The traditional combination of materials in the bridge is a maple base and an ebony top. Other stable woods that have a specific gravity close to .73—or that of medium-density maple—are also quite effective.

The grain orientation of a banjo bridge is also important. As viewed from the end of the bridge, the grain lines should be parallel to the head and about 1/16" to 1/8" apart.

Break Angle

If a banjo were a car, the engine would be the bridge, and the carburetor would be adjustment of the angle which the strings break over the bridge. You may change this angle on most banjos by simply moving the leading edge of the tailpiece up or down in relation to the head. Better tailpieces have an adjustment screw on the back of the tailpiece for this purpose. As a general rule, increase break angle when you increase bridge weight. Also, remember that a taller bridge will automatically give a greater break angle. Some experimentation will be needed whenever you set up your banjo with a new bridge. More is said on break angle in future pages.

The point to grasp here is that every part of the banjo contributes or somehow affects its sound. Even the instrument with the tightest and best-fitting parts won't be at its best unless it is set up by one who understands how its parts effect the dynamics of banjo sound. Thus begins the journey into the mysteries of the banjo system.

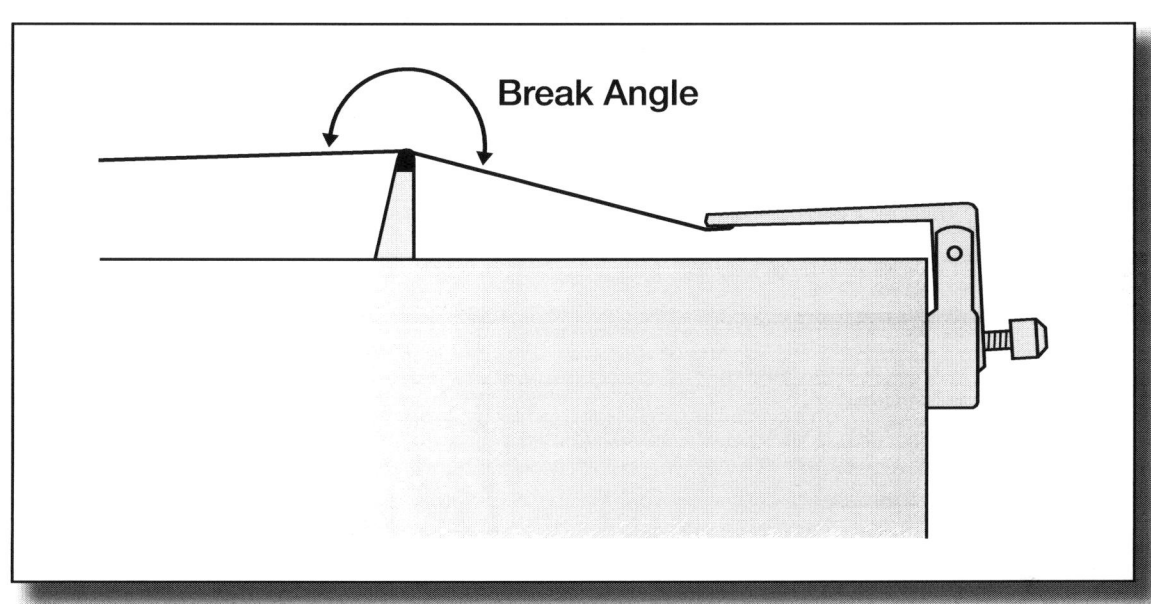

Chapter Three
Warming Up Your Banjo

Does your banjo have an overly bright sound or a harsh edge? Do other musicians cringe at your attempts to blend in musically? In my many years of doing professional banjo set-up, I have found this tone problem to be quite common. Typical banjo sound contains a high overtone content. To explain further, the thin responsive head on the banjo allows the strings' subvibrations, or overtones, to become audible. The high harmonic content of the banjo's sound in fact defines the unique quality of its tone. But even if your banjo is loud, it doesn't necessarily mean that it is sounding its best. I'd say that the sound that loud banjos produce contains a large measure of what our ears perceive as "noise." The heavy metal-laden banjo machine tends to serve up more than its share of high frequency resonance, and if we are not careful, distorted harmonics from improper intonation could be particularly irritating.

Naturally, we all have slightly different ideas of good sound, but among serious musicians, most favor a certain warmth of tone. The secret to finding this warm quality in your banjo is to try to free up some of its lower frequencies while controlling its high overtones from becoming overpowering. The most pleasant tones to the human ear tend to be in the medium to lower frequency range. Most banjos are capable of producing these frequencies, but they are often choked off by a set-up that is too tight and which restricts the banjo's bass potential. When bass is present, it rounds out the sound and helps buffer the high frequency noise. Hopefully the following information will assist in achieving even and balanced tone on whatever style of banjo you have.

If you have a Heli-mount style banjo, perfectly even tension is automatically applied to the banjo head. This new design replaces upwards of seventy pieces of metal hardware, and mounts the tone components independent of direct metal contact, producing fuller, deeper, and more even tone with less work. Detailed set-up advice follows for adding a musical warmth to whatever kind of banjo you have.

Heads

So how do we encourage the bass and control the noise? The common first remedy is to loosen the head. I won't go into detail as how to do this, since if you have gotten this far in the book I must assume you have the tool and know-how for that. I'd suggest using the right size nut driver, usually 1/4". Make sure all nuts have equal tension and the tension hoop remains straight. If the instrument loses too much volume or brilliance with a looser head, you may want to experiment with different heads.

Some players of overly bright banjos have installed a "Fiberskin" head. This is a simulated natural skin-looking head that is a little thicker. It can be an effective way to muffle the highest frequencies and it is a particularly common replacement head on Stelling banjos. We are always walking a tightrope with adjustments on a banjo. The danger is that the Fiberskin may cause the instrument to sound lifeless and dull. If you tighten the head too much you might choke off the musicality altogether, especially with 11-inch heads. In most traditional banjos, you are better off with a Renaissance head or a regular frosted head. "5-Star" heads seem a little heavier but tend to sound a little icier than standard Remo frosted heads. Clear heads, which can be sharp and edgy in a traditional banjo, sound their best evenly tight or helically-mounted. See more details on heads in succeeding chapters.

Fiber Skin Head on homemade Old-Time banjo

Bridges

The banjo bridge is a source of much myth and misunderstanding. There are many features to the bridge that can distract from or add to optimal banjo sound. It's important to pay attention to the following bridge features to help limit unwanted noise, yet allow ample volume.

Bridge Weight

This is the most crucial factor in bridges. Most bridges are too light, and while they translate the string vibration into a bright sound, they also allow audible responsiveness to unwanted overtones. On 5-string banjos the bridge should weigh no less than two grams, and under three grams.

String Slots

If the string slots are not cut to fit the string snugly, or if the front edge of the slot is too deep, noise can occur. A bridge with a wide ebony top for extra weight, and longer contact area between the string and the bridge, is the most effective. Be sure the playing side of the string slot makes sharp, intimate contact with the string for clean tone.

Bridge Height

With a hook and nut style banjo, it is important to use only the bridge height which is optimal for the instrument. This can vary slightly with each banjo. Different heights will produce different tone results, but changing the bridge height obviously affects the string action and resulting playability. It's recommended to avoid over-tightening of the banjo's coordinator rods in order to force a banjo to accept a different height bridge. This can cause unwanted stresses, bad sound, and potential damage to the banjo pot. This can also contribute to harshness and unwanted bass constriction. To find the proper height, remove the strings, loosen the coordinator nuts by the tailpiece side of the rim, check the evenness of head tension, tighten the neck to the rim first, and then hand-tighten the nuts on the tailpiece side of the rim. Then re-string the banjo and find a bridge high enough so no strings rattle or buzz anywhere on the neck.

Tailpieces

Another important part that should be considered when attempting to warm up a banjo's sound is its tailpiece. This part exerts the downward pressure of the strings on the bridge and head. Just as it is important to determine a banjo's "natural" bridge height, it is also necessary to seek a tailpiece position that is rigid, yet which allows the natural vibration of the bridge and head.

There is always an interplay of offsetting factors, but the following guidelines are generally true. With 5/8" bridges I like to fasten the Presto tailpiece rigidly down and touching the tension hoop, but pointing up toward the top of the bridge. Of course the higher the bridge, the higher the tailpiece should be. If there is a screw in the end of the tailpiece, I would remove it so that there is solid contact with the side of the tension hoop. Kershner and Price tailpieces are a bit more solid so they allow for a little more leeway in how they are set up. For example, they can be off the top of the tension hoop a little and be parallel to the head, or even pointing up a little.

Beware of too much choking down at the tailpiece. If you need to crank down on the tailpiece to get any life out of the instrument, you probably have other weak links in the banjo system that should be addressed first.

Nechville and Stelling tailpieces are pre-set by their anchoring points on the tension hoop, but still allow some down pressure adjustment. These tailpieces also give a bit of side-to-side adjustment for sting centering.

Nechville Tailpiece

Summary

Whenever working on your banjo, remember that small changes add up to a combined result that is often quite noticeable. When facing a choice for which adjustments to make to warm your sound, opt for making several small adjustments rather than one large one. Banjos usually respond better to many minute adjustments rather than to one drastic one.

Chapter Four
Heading for Great Sound

The flexible head is the sound board of the banjo. Just as quarter-sawn spruce is the material of choice for guitar sound boards, polyester film (otherwise known as mylar) is the material of choice for modern banjo sound boards. This is the banjo component that is actively engaged in pumping sound waves into the air. The acoustic properties of the head are what give the banjo its characteristic sound.

There are basically three types of banjo heads—mylar (polyester plastic), imitation skin (Fiberskin), and natural skin. The widest and most common family of heads is the mylar group. These can be further separated into coated and non-coated groups.

Most heads are coated on the top surface with a rather heavy coating of white textured pigment. The purpose of the coating is three-fold. First, it looks appropriate for the banjo. Next, it provides a non-slip surface for the right hand and bridge. Most importantly, it diffuses the sound somewhat and helps remove the naked harshness of a clear plastic head. Of the white coated heads, the two most common brands are Remo and 5-Star (or Ludwig heads).

Remo Heads

The Remo head is used by most banjo builders and is the most common brand. The regular Remo head is inexpensive and commonly used by major manufacturers. They generally produce a bright, crisp sound that grabs the attention of many banjo buyers.

The Remo head has become a standard by which we judge other heads. To avoid confusion, the exact head that we are talking about is the 1100 M1 medium crown, frosted top side. (One benefit associated with Remo heads is the wide variety of options available in sizes and coatings.)

However, the frosting on the Remo head is somewhat susceptible to scratching off. To help alleviate this problem, you may lightly sand the surface of the Remo head with 400-grit sandpaper. This will remove the high, rough nodules that tend to break off and scratch across the head—especially during bridge replacement.

The oldest Remo heads had a more durable coating, but Remo changed their coating process (I believe in the 80's) and have only recently formulated a more durable coating. Most of us banjo players are used to scratched, worn-out looking heads, but Remo has another solution: Why not put the frosting on the underside of the head? It's still white in appearance and should sound similar, but will not scratch off.

I like this idea, although I do not like the shiny appearance of the smooth Mylar top. However, the old 400-grit sandpaper comes in handy again! I simply remove the shine by sanding the top surface, and the head looses its overly shiny appearance.

Remo will make various sizes of heads to fit almost any banjo and also offers three different crown heights. The crown height is the tallness of the head. Use a high crown if you have short bracket hooks, and use a low crown if you have an arch-top tone ring. Medium crowns work the best on most bluegrass banjos.

The Remo head is constructed by perforating the perimeter of the Mylar head material and bonding it with epoxy into an aluminum channel bent into a hoop. The epoxy fills in the hoop and sometimes overfills it, leaving a high ramp of glue around the seating surface of the head. Be careful that the epoxy is not unevenly high or it may tend to cause an uneven installation.

5-Star Heads

5-Star heads are constructed differently. First, they are made with a slightly stretchy Mylar, but the coating is much thicker and more durable than that of the Remo head. The perimeter of the head material is not glued in, but is crimped into a steel band, and it is virtually impossible to pull it apart. There is not as much variety offered with 5-Star heads, but generally they are a good choice for a bright, dry tone, which means a clear sound with a little less sustain.

5-Star, as well as Remo, offers both clear and non-frosted white heads. The tonal characteristics of the clear heads tend to be similar, producing maximum brilliance and transparency of tone. (By transparency, I mean that no overtones are masked and more of the high harmonics are amplified.) When newly installed, clear heads can be very striking looking, but they lose their clarity somewhat with use. In a traditional banjo, most experienced players shy away from them because they mask no overtones and often sound too bright or shrill to the ears. Again, here is an opportunity to point out that the different construction of helically-mounted banjos may be a big benefit to lovers of clear heads due to less metallic interference present in the Heli-Mount design.

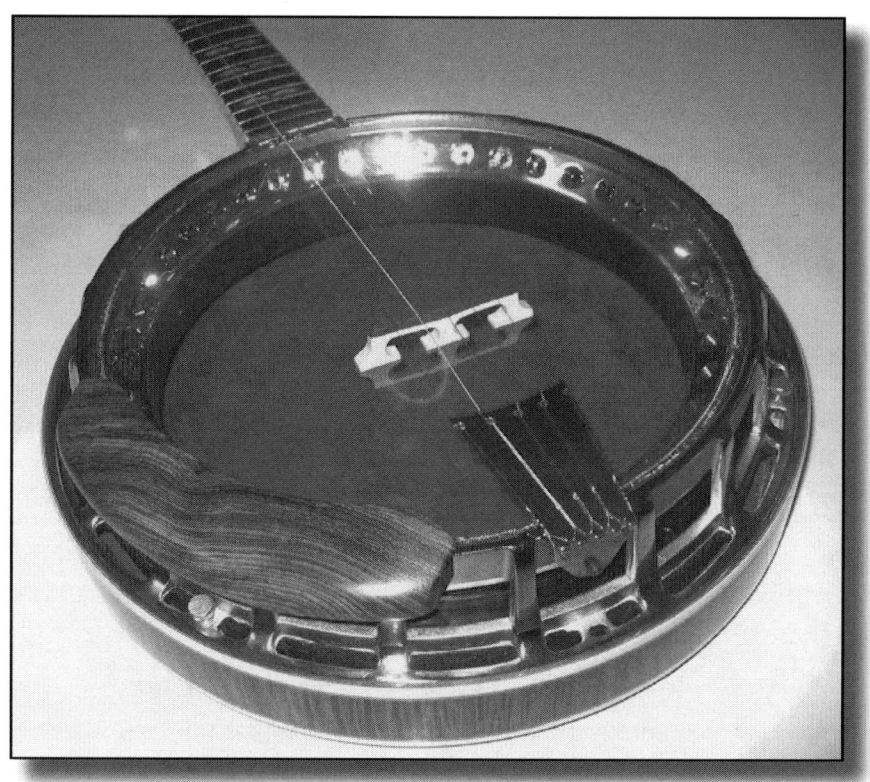

Heading My Way

If you have read this far, you are probably ready for some hot set-up tips related to heads. One reason I like the banjo is that the sound board is never stuck at just one stiffness like on a guitar or any other wood bodied instrument. Since the head is the sound board of the banjo, any adjustment of its stiffness or tension will greatly affect the way the instrument sounds.

Head Tightening

A conventional banjo has 24 nuts and hooks to tighten (with a two-part Heli-Mount frame, even head tightening is automatic). All banjo enthusiasts recognize the importance of getting even tension on each nut and hook around the perimeter of the banjo. Some have even gone to the trouble to use a torque wrench to equalize the force required to turn each nut. It is possible that you'll be working with an older banjo so beware of sticky or rusty hooks and nuts. If you are using a torque wrench, you may be getting totally different actual tension on each nut. If you are starting from scratch and have your banjo completely apart, you can check each nut for free turning before reassembling your banjo. You'll have to install a few hooks and nuts across from each other first to keep the tension hoop level, and work up to having all of the hooks and nuts snugged up evenly first by squeezing the tension hoop down and just thumb tightening the nuts all the way around. I then use a ¼" nut driver, or whatever size is required, to travel around the perimeter. The first go around will take about a full turn and the next go around, probably a half tun, and successive trips around the perimeter you will only tighten in ¼ turn increments until the head is up to proper pitch.

I tune the head to G♯ for most 11" flat head banjos. While this is widely considered the ideal tension, it is difficult to hear that pitch coming from the head. You must first tune the banjo perfectly with a tuner, then tap lightly on the head and try to isolate a note and sing along with it. Then try listening to that note on the banjo. I usually play my 5th string and compare it to the note I think I hear on the head. I try the 6th and 7th frets on the first string and see if I hear any of those tones coming from the tapping or scratching on the head. Sometimes it is easier to hear what I believe is the head's harmonic frequency, or a high whisp of a sound that is an octave higher than you would expect. When I am reasonably sure of the head's pitch, I make adjustments to go in the direction of G♯ and re-test. If it's reasonably tight to the feel, it's likely that you will be close to the G♯ already. If you are way off, try listening for a different note, because you are probably picking up the resonant frequency of the pot or some other acoustic property of the banjo. When you are reasonably sure that you have picked out the head's initial pitch, go in one-quarter turns of the wrench until you arrive at G♯. I have also had some success setting an Intelli IMT-500 or IMT 900 on the head's surface, and while lightly touching the strings and tapping gently on the bridge, the tuner will tell you a pitch. After several attempts yielding a common reading, you can assume the tuner is giving you the actual pitch of the head. A more reliable method is to use a calibrated drum dial indicator and place it on the head about 1 ½ inches from the tone ring. If the needle comes up to about 90 or 91 on the dial, it is probably very close to that magic G♯.

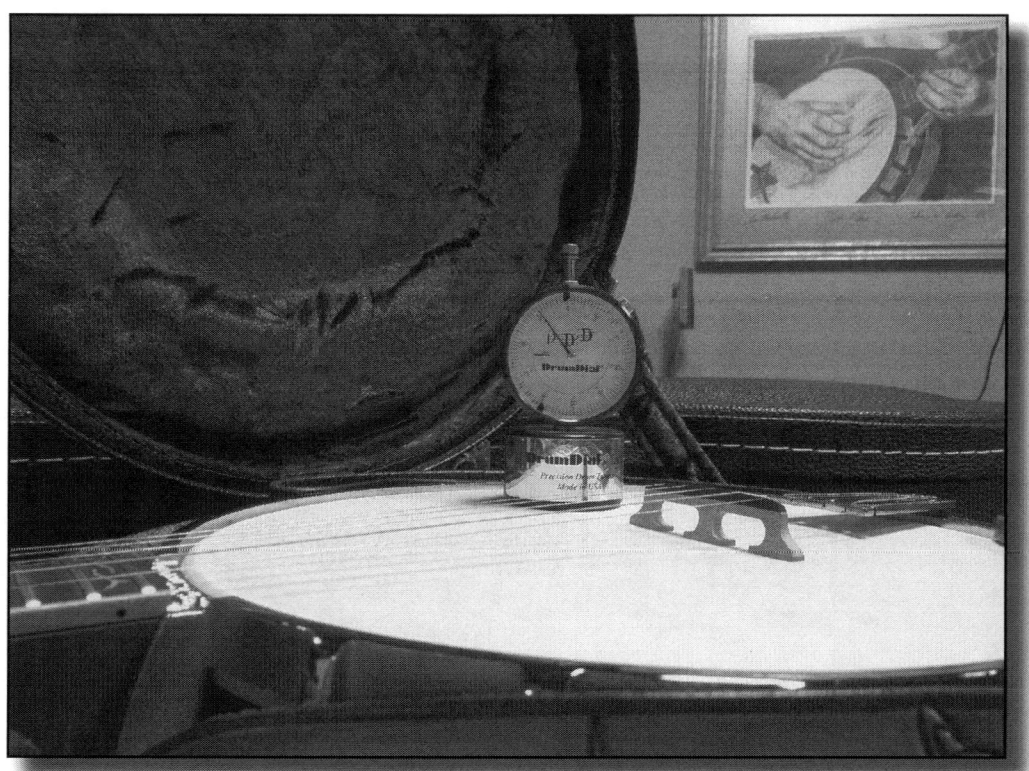

Checking head tension with a Drum Dial

Plan to spend a fair amount of time on a conventional hook and nut banjo getting the evenness of each part the same and up to pitch. If you have a Heli-Mount banjo, you might hear the pitch change if someone taps the head while you are turning the tensioning wrenches.

If you are installing or re-installing a head, you have the opportunity to noticeably improve the look of your banjo. The dull appearance of the edge bead of the banjo head can be sanded and buffed to a shine if you have the proper equipment. If you want to simulate a gold look you can get reasonably close by coloring the polished edge bead with a wood-colored permanent marker.

If you are as picky about tone as I am, you can inspect the head's glue ridge (if it's a Remo), and make sure it is not preventing an intimate metal-to-metal contact where the head's metal bead touches the tension hoop. I have even tried filing down the high spots, but this is a good way to waste a head, because it's so easy to abrade and weaken the head right at the critical strength zone. With 5-Star heads I have considered further crimping the bead down upon the Mylar if it looked like it was loosely crimped. If you notice such a thing, you should choose a different head before going to the extreme of putting the head in a vice or hammering the bead flat all the way around.

My rule of thumb is: Avoid sound-absorbing gaps. For example, if you have used the Remo idea of a frosted-inside head, then you have the rough white paint in contact with the smooth top surface of your tone ring. With a little settling in under head tension, the paint will flatten out and you will have no sound-absorbing gaps. The mere possibility, however, that microscopic gaps do exist is enough for me to take the easy precaution of smoothing the inside contact area of the head with 1000 or 600-grit sandpaper. Many of the small set-up tricks I use will have negligible effect upon tone, but again, added together as a whole, the cumulative effect is noticeable.

Heading for Tradition

For some early classic recordings of Earl Scruggs, he had a natural skin head on his banjo. The drawback to natural skin is its stretching with humidity, but if you are able to keep it tight through frequent adjustment, you'd probably like the sound. The high flexibility of a skin head tends to allow clarity of a wide harmonic range, which results in a very sweet tone. If tight, it will be bright but with less sustain than a plastic head, lending a "drier" quality to the sound.

A good compromise between a skin head and a plastic head is the Fiberskin head made by Remo. With this head, you won't have the problem with weather changes, and you will retain some of the sonic properties of a skin head. Regular Fiberskin heads are actually Mylar heads laminated with a fibrous material similar to "Tyvec" house wrap. These heads are a little thicker and come in two weights. I prefer the thinner one. I like the fiberskin especially on 6 string banjos, and on 12" open back banjos.

Fiber-Skin Head from Remo

Heading for Expression

I am surprised how few people use their banjo head for displaying some kind of art work. The banjo head seems a perfect place to post a message or decorative statement. Why not color your head or draw a design directly on its surface with permanent markers? A light coat of a clear spray lacquer may help seal the artwork, but beware it also may cause bleeding of colors. Don't worry, however, replacement heads are available from us and most music stores, so have fun. Solid black heads with shiny or dull appearances are available, but they usually require extra tightening to get the best sound.

It is also possible to find reflective flashy novelty heads that are ready for installation. If you are starved for attention these heads are capable of aiming blinding laser beams at innocent outdoor spectators. These are simply mylar heads laminated with a layer of decorative shiny film. These heads tend to be a little thicker and therefore less responsive to the high frequencies. If you are seeking to take a sharp edge off the tone and you like the look, this could help.

Electric Heads?

For the renegade types, Nechville makes several amplifying options available, especially for owners of Helimount banjos. The modular nature of the Helimount style banjo enables an easy switch to a new class of heads designed for electrifying your banjo sound. The Turbo module is one such idea that converts an acoustic banjo into an electric banjo. It replaces the tone ring and regular 11" head with an 11" thin wooden head. The Turbo has a small 6" head and volume and tone controls all mounted on this wood head. It maintains its banjo tone and can be amplified to rock concert volume. Creative banjoists may opt to eliminate the head membrane altogether. A solid top with magnetic pickups can easily be installed in the same manner. This defines Nechville's solid body Quasar module, which produces a powerful electric guitar type of tone.

Turbo Module mounted in Corona Heli-mount frame

Chapter Five
"Magic" Bridges

An experienced banjo player knows that there is something "magical" about a good banjo bridge. You have probably tested identical-looking bridges and wondered why there are sometimes big differences in tone between them. Now with all of the varieties of bridges on the market and with everyone making big claims about their various merits, it is worth considering bridge features that affect banjo tone, features that improve banjo playability, and features that are good ideas from a structural and functional standpoint.

Common sense dictates that a bridge needs to be strong enough to prevent breaking and/or excessive sagging under string tension. A slight tilt back toward the tailpiece not only helps prevent tipping, but it bisects the break angle and optimizes the perpendicularity of the strings' downward pressure on the bridge. The customary ebony top serves primarily the utilitarian purpose of providing a hard surface that will not easily wear out from string tension, and that gives the top edge more strength so as to prevent collapsing. Maple is commonly used for bridges because it seems to have the right combination of strength, stiffness, and density, and it's readily available.

Another functional feature that is absolutely essential for 5-string professional banjos is scale length compensation. The need for compensation varies with the heaviness of the strings and their distance from the frets. Need for compensation is especially pronounced on the non-wound third string. With conventional 5-string set ups, the third string slot should be about 3/32" further back, toward the tailpiece, from the rest of the strings. Some makers, notably Stelling, has addressed the compensation issue from the standpoint of the nut by shortening the 3rd string scale at the nut end compared to the 2nd string. This means that the 3rd string plays a bit flat when fretted, improving compensation in theory. The addition of a Nechville compensated Enterprise Bridge usually corrects intonation altogether.

A banjo with an arched or radiused fingerboard needs to have a bridge with a radiused top edge. Most bridge makers, however, fail to realize that a slight radius to the top edge is beneficial even with regular flat frets. When struck, the heavier 3rd and 4th strings take a little more room to vibrate. Therefore, higher action is preferred for them to prevent rattles and choked tone. Also, it seems a little bit easier to hit the center strings when they are resting a little higher. The added arch helps fight a bridge's tendency to sag over time as well, but beware of the increased need for 3rd string compensation when using a radiused bridge with a flat fingerboard.

For easiest playability, string spacing and bridge height should be based on personal preference according to hand size and playing technique. In themselves, neither factor really affects tone. Sloppy string slots can sometimes be a source of dirty sound, but this subject will be discussed in the chapter on set-up. There is a general trend to use taller bridges whenever possible, for their beneficial effect upon good tone and volume.

Changing the bridge height affects the banjo sound because usually the mass of the bridge changes as does the break angle over the bridge. The higher the bridge, the more downward pressure is directed down on the head. Try to imagine a ridiculously high bridge with the strings forming a sharp break angle over its top. It's easy to imagine that much more of the strings' tension is being used to pull the bridge directly down into the head. Cranking down the tailpiece has essentially the same effect of increasing the break angle and resultant downward pressure on the head. Both affect the tone similarly to tightening the head of the banjo. Of course, this becomes a balancing act, and there comes a point where more break angle diminishes the instrument's warmth and tonal subtleties.

If you are installing a higher bridge, and wish to encourage a warmer sound, raise up the leading edge of the tailpiece the same amount as the increase in bridge height, to keep the break angle as it was with the shorter bridge. See the chapter on tailpieces for more detail on this subject.

Perhaps the biggest factor in finding a magic bridge is to find the magic weight. Most inexpensive bridges are too light to serve the purposes of professional players. A thin, light bridge causes the banjo head to respond actively to high overtones and high frequency noise. The banjo may be bright, but difficult to work with in recording or over a PA system. If a bridge is too heavy, it will reduce volume and produce a darker tone, with more sustain.

From experimenting with bridges for many years, I have found that the most common bridge of maple topped with ebony still seems to produce the most reliable results. Since wood varies tremendously from tree to tree—and even from different parts of the same board—it is critical for the bridge builder to be extremely careful in choosing and cutting his raw materials. Many new bridges are being sold these days and it is generally a gamble when buying a bridge and installing it yourself. Considering these inconsistencies and the less-than perfect designs offered by most bridge builders, you might have to try a dozen bridges before you hit one that is magic. Among the many maple and ebony bridges on the market, the Enterprise Bridge is made with consistent high quality, is precision compensated, weighed, and measured, and comes in any height over 9/16".

Maple is not the only material that is suitable for bridges. The density of wood is expressed as its specific gravity. The specific gravity of bridge wood is close to .73. Some hardwoods that have specific gravities slightly less than average maple actually tend to act like noise filters.

Words are inefficient to describe sound accurately, but I offer the following characterstics of banjo sound and list bridge features that would affect tone toward that result.

Musicality

This is the elusive "magic" tone that we all dream about. It is the bottom line...our goal. Musicality is likely the result of all the many set-up features being right at the same time. I would define it as a nice rounded edge to the note with good note separation, yet adequate sustain and bass response. Specifically relating to the bridge, I would suggest using a bridge of medium density maple with slightly bigger feet in contact with the head. If I were able to choose my bridge height as on an adjustable neck Helimount, I would opt for a tall bridge, about 3/4" but have it thinned down to weigh about 2.5 or 2.6 grams. If you have a standard banjo and are following my set-up guidelines, you may not be able to use such a high bridge, in which case an 11/16", 2.4 gram Enterprise compensated bridge would be optimal.

Sustain

Some banjoists will say that a banjo should not have too much sustain. Their problem stems from notes ringing on top of each other and muddying up their tone. In some cases, and for some styles, this may be a valid argument. However, for my taste, I would say that the more sustain, the better.

Quick-picking guitarists do not seem to have a problem with sustain, so why should a banjo not sustain? The answer might be that a lingering banjo sustain is usually not very musical. Rather than a full-bodied pleasant sustain, we normally hear nothing but big harmonic overtones that can sound harsh or ringy. However, I cherish the musical richness of a more full-bodied and smooth sustain.

A heavier bridge makes a crucial difference in approaching this ideal. If you can get all of the setup factors working together with a heavier bridge (2.4 to 3 grams), you could open up some new musical horizons for yourself.

Chimes and Bell-like Tone

The treble end adds life to the tone, but it must be presented in a balanced way for optimal sound. Besides the mass being right, it is essential that the bridge is in the right position on the banjo head and that it has the proper intonation.

When all of the strings have good intonation, the sympathetic vibrations from all of the non-picked strings will also supplement the harmonic content of the note. The break angle over the bridge should be just enough to bring out the highs. The simplest way to hear if your highs are working is to hit the 21st fret and to listen for a nice sustain. Then try the harmonic test.

Starting with the 12th fret 1st harmonic, touch the 1st string lightly, directly above the 12th fret without actually contacting the fret. Then pick the string while immediately releasing contact with the string. You should hear the harmonic chime of a bell like tone. If the harmonic chime is clear and loud, that's good. Try the chime on all the strings at the 12th fret, then find other harmonics at the 19th, 7th, 5th, 4th and so on. Now you can recheck the placement of your bridge by fretting behind the 12th fret and comparing the note struck with the previous chime. As you know by now, if the bridge is out of place, the fretted note will be a different pitch than the chime, and you'll have to move your bridge or suffer from harmonic distortion and a noisy, out of tune banjo. See the set-up chapter for fine-tuning the bridge placement. If you are wishing to accentuate more of a harmonic content to your sound, try using a compensated bridge with a thinner, relatively sharp leading edge. You also may consider a bridge that weighs closer to 2 grams.

Bass Response

Professional players are always looking for great bass response from their instruments. There is a continuing trend to deepen and broaden the banjo sound. The right bridge of at least 2.5 grams will take you partly there, but moderate head tension and a tailpiece that points slightly upward will help too.

Wide Sound

A balanced tone with lots of nice highs, mids, and lows has what is called a "wide sound." If there is overall balance, the highs will not stick out and sound ragged, and you will be glad to hear the sustain. Unmasked highs sound piercing and thin, while lows alone without the balancing effect of treble would be lifeless and dull. I believe that completely even head tension will assist in widening the sound.

The Nechville Enterprise Bridge, in addition to being precision-weighed, is a fully compensated bridge, which allows for extremely accurate intonation with medium or light gauge strings. Each bridge is made from woods which have been tested for proper density and tone characteristics. Its unique slightly "S" shape maximizes its stability under string tension and optimizes vibrational transfer to the banjo head. It also has more mass along its top edge to prevent sagging, and has an arched top surface which improves playability and decreases the possibility of fret noise.

While changing bridges may make a significant difference in your banjo sound, it is essential to continue keeping in mind your instrument's "wholistic" nature. Even the best of bridges is but one component of the overall system of sound produced by your banjo.

Chapter Six
Tailpiece Adjustments

Tailpiece adjustments alone will usually produce predictable results, but it is essential to keep in mind that altering bridge height, string gauge, and head tension can limit or reverse the effects of the tailpiece adjustment.

There are several types of banjo tailpieces. Simple string-anchoring tailpieces on inexpensive and old-time banjos are almost always non-adjustable, but they do one important thing well: They anchor the strings solidly on or near the tension hoop. Since there is no extension toward the bridge adding downward pressure on the head, the effect upon the system is that of loosening the head and minimizing the break angle over the bridge. Generally, this will lead to a darker and more open tone.

Presto tailpieces are the most common type of tailpiece used on Mastertone type banjos. There are at least two variations of this tailpiece design—one being adjustable up and down, and the other not. Speaking in general terms (as specific results will depend on the individual banjo's whole system), this type of tailpiece traditionally should not need to be adjustable.

If an adjustable Presto tailpiece is angled down too far, it usually sounds bad. The reason for this is that the Presto is not a very solid tailpiece. When it is cranked down, it creates a weak link in the system. It is desirable with a Presto to keep it pointing to the top of the bridge to avoid what might become a "sound sponge" if trying to add too much break angle.

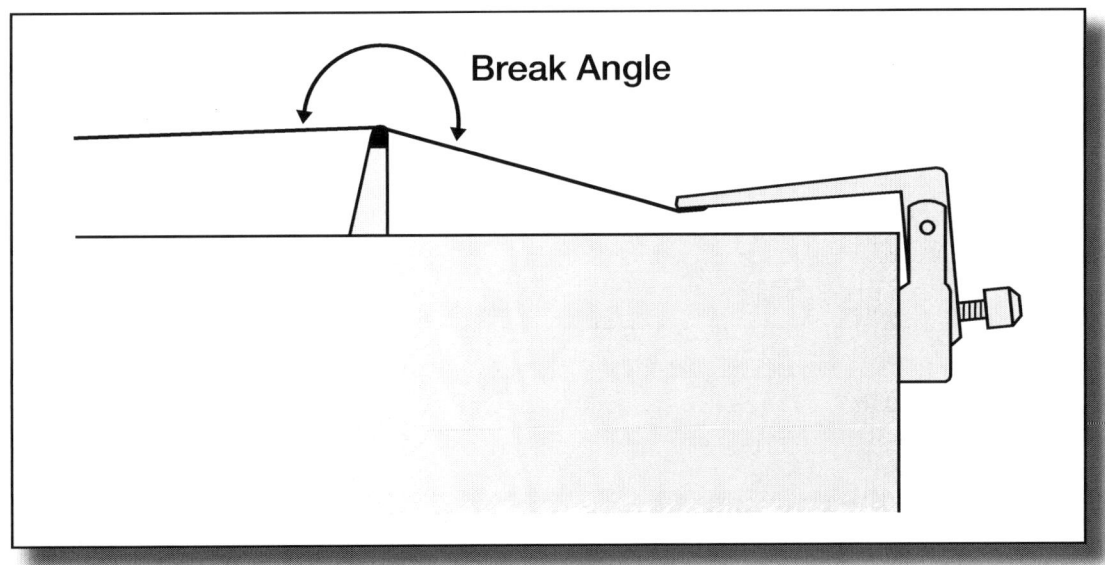

A weak link caused by tailpiece down pressure

With a taller bridge, you may want to have the tailpiece up, away from the tension hoop, and actually bend or point it up a bit to avoid the "weak link" syndrome. The danger of this approach is that the higher tailpiece is less stable and more susceptible to knocking out of tune more easily. One more simple trick is to put an extra nut on the Presto tailpiece anchor bolt on the top side of the flange to give a little more rigidity to the tailpiece.

Kershner tailpieces are a little more rigid, so you have more flexibility in deciding how far to crank them down. As a general rule, crank down on low bridges and leave the tailpiece high with higher bridges. Kershner tailpieces generally sound best just a bit off the tension hoop and pointing straight parallel to the head, or pointing up for high bridges.

Types of Tailpieces

Price and Nechville tailpieces are wider and a little heavier than the other tailpieces on the market, so they have the advantage of rigidity like the Kershner. Other advantages of the Price and Nechville styles are easy string changing and "in-line" string spacing. The in-line effect is important because it keeps the break angle pointing straight toward the head, thus losing no energy to sideways pull on the bridge.

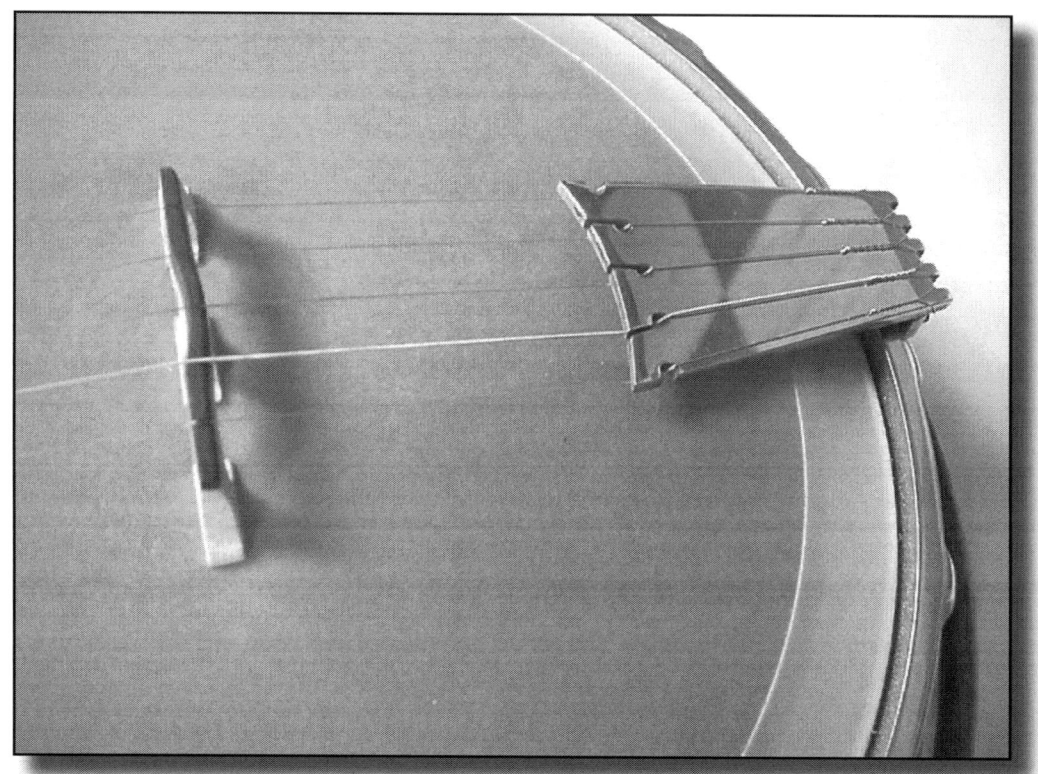

Properly adjusted Nechville Tailpiece

While I believe that the in-line tailpiece feature is an important factor, most people will not be able to tell a difference in tone (if that is the only factor considered). The Price and Nechville tailpieces are engineered to give slightly lower break angle on the middle strings, which helps distribute string tension more evenly on the bridge and head. Nechville's also includes anchor points that give added stability against lateral rocking.

Considering all the most important features of tailpieces, Nechville has designed a tailpiece similar to Price's that has no bolt and nut attachment. It stays on only with string tension, and is easy to remove with loosened string tension.

There are many other types of tailpieces, some even with individually adjustable fingers. Generally if you can fix the tailpiece firmly without rocking, most tailpieces can work well. For me, the most important features are easy string changing, and stability against lateral rocking, to keep the strings in tune.

Chapter Seven
Tone Rings

Much of the defining character of a banjo's sound comes from the type of tone ring employed in its construction. The tone ring is the ring that the head is stretched over, and it is usually made out of metal.

You must not get the tone ring confused with the part called the rim. In good bluegrass banjos, the metal tone ring sits on top of the wooden rim. In other banjos, however, there may not be a separate tone ring and rim. In this case, you might hear the words "rim," "tone ring," "shell," "frame," "pot," or "body" used interchangeably. If we are talking about a one piece tone ring/rim, I'll call it a "tone rim."

You'll see references to tone rings all throughout this book, so I'll limit my discussion to the basic types of tone rings, and some ideas as to what you might be able to do with your tone ring if there seems to be a problem with it.

Aluminum-Bodied Banjos

Let's start with the basic one piece tone rim made of aluminum. You have all probably owned an aluminum-shelled banjo early on in your playing career. These are inexpensive imported banjos from the far east, and some may now even come from Singapore or Malaysia. From a design perspective, these banjos are a great design. There are few parts, they are light weight, they are adjustable, and they sound remarkably good when set up correctly. Many advanced players will dismiss this design as having no merit for a bluegrass player, but if you are a beginner, these banjos are often the best deal, especially if you can do some basic set-up work.

The aluminum shell is attached to the neck via one coordinator rod. In order to set up this type of banjo to sound its best, make sure the neck is attached snugly and that the rod is causing the neck to tilt back at the customary 3 degree angle, so that when the bridge is installed, the string action will not be too high. There is usually plenty of adjustment available in this rod to accommodate different bridge heights. Ideally, as outlined in the professional setup article to come, you don't want to put too much stress on the pot or you will warp it out of round and effect the tone, but I would say on a one-piece tone rim banjo, the priority is to get good playability, even at the expense of some slight warping of the tone rim. Be careful, however, because some cheaper aluminum bodies can completely be folded up by over-adjustment.

Once the rod is secured, check all the tension nuts. Sometimes on these cheap banjos the nuts get rusty or stuck and may be loose, even though they do not turn easily. You may need to hold the tensioning hook with a pliers to prevent it from turning and popping off the tension hoop. Try to get the head evenly tight all around by checking the head for soft spots. When everything is tight, you may install a good bridge and follow the guidelines in the other set-up chapters to complete the job.

Old-time Tone Rings

Many earlier banjos had wooden hoops for rims and then employed a simple circle of brass wire as a tone ring. Usually the brass ring would be welded together to form a continuous hoop. This type of configuration is common on many early banjos such as the Gibson RB, TB, or PB 1, 2, or 11 banjos.

An advancement to the simple rolled rod tone ring was the Vega White Ladie tone ring that is still popular on many old-time and open-back banjos. A combination of a brass rod, a scalloped hoop and a spun retaining shroud gives this ring an added complexity and delivers a bit more complexity to the tone as well. It has a pretty and sweet tone but this ring is not capable of maximum volume and projection, because it's relatively light design does not give it a strong inertial mass as described above. The three elements of this ring increase the likelihood of sound-absorbing gaps or structural deficiencies that may rob sound.

Spun Tone Rings

Plectrum and tenor banjoists are more familiar with spun rings, as they were employed on the Bacon and Day Silver Belle and other popular 4-string models. Rather than casting or mechanically rolling metal into a hoop, the Silver Belle rings were spun into shape over a pattern on a spinning lathe. During manufacturing, the metal is not cut to shape as on a regular metal lathe but is soft enough to be pushed into shape, almost like throwing a clay pot on a potter's wheel. The resulting product is a very thin and relatively light tone ring that is usually used in conjunction with a rolled brass wire hoop. The hoop makes contact with the wooden rim and the inside of the spun ring makes contact with the brass hoop. With the spun ring mounted upon such a hard surface as the brass ring, the spun ring can be much more active acoustically than a tone ring that is mechanically dampened by the direct contact to the wood. The spun ring did not gain much favor with 5-string players, because they favored the hard-hitting sound of a more massive ring.

The Mastertone Rings

I guess that it was in the 1930s when Gibson began to use heavy cast brass or bronze tone rings in their high quality banjos. There are two basic cast rings that were and still are employed on bluegrass banjos, the arch top tone ring and the flat head tone ring.

Archtop Tone Rings

Archtop rings have a different profile than the flat head. The effective area of head vibration is smaller and therefore produces a brighter sound. They also have a bit less mass than the flat head ring. Some original archtops had springs with ball bearings under the tone ring which may have been an attempt to help keep the calfskin head tight through humidity changes, but it also served as a bell mounting to give the tone ring additional resonance. The famous luthier Lloyd Loar had some influence on the ball bearing design, noting that the hard surfaces of the bearings would give a more bell-like resonance to the tone. This is also the precursor to Nechville's Cyclotronic tone ring which you'll hear about shortly.

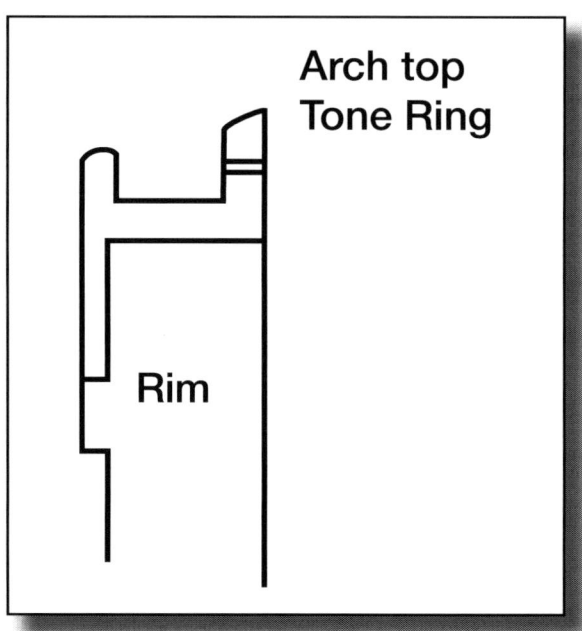

Flat Head Tone Rings

Most bluegrass banjos today have heavy cast and machined brass or bronze flat head tone rings. Pre-war flat head tone rings are extremely rare, and consequently highly sought-after. As explained in an earlier chapter, tone ring formulations vary widely from one banjo to the next, but they all are made from some type of copper alloy such as bronze. Makers would often refer to the tone ring material as "bell bronze," but this term normally refers to a formula of 80% copper and 20% tin. Pre-war formulas were inexact and showed some variations in material.

The standard manufacturing method is to sand-cast tone ring blanks, and then machine them down to final dimensions. They weigh between 3 and 4 pounds and offer a high inertial mass, meaning that when a head is stretched upon it, the massiveness of the tone ring serves to allow more and longer vibration of the plucked strings.

Consequently, the Mastertone flat head ring is now the accepted standard for three-finger picking. With some minor alterations, all of the major banjo makers today are using a ring that resembles this design.

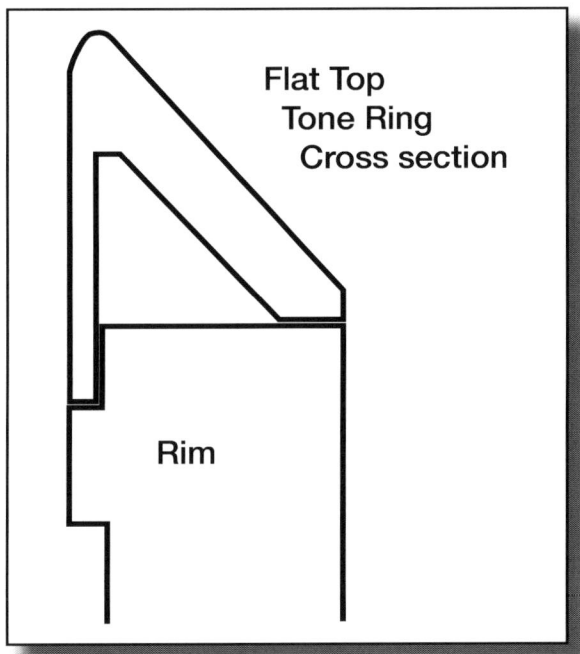

You may have heard of "centrifugally cast" tone rings, made popular by the late Richard Kulesh. This method of casting produces uniformly dense, high quality castings, but generally require more machining after casting and therefore are more expensive. Certain makers have tried to reformulate 1930's rings in their own small smelting operations with some success.

Problems with Tone Rings

If you have tried everything you can think of and your banjo still doesn't sound right, you may have a tone ring problem. In my opinion, it's rare to find a problem with the tone ring itself, but it's far more common to find a problem with the rim or between the tone ring and rim. I have found that all tone rings, if massive enough and fit well to a good rim, will sound good. The slight variance in tone nuances that you might sense when changing to a centrifugally cast ring for example, could be just as much due to the different fit of the tone ring upon the rim. Or you may find that when the banjo is reassembled, the changed set-up factors of head tension, bridge placement, coordinator rod tension, etc, have done more to alter sound than the new tone ring.

Many banjos just don't have the proper fit between the tone ring and rim. I have even seen factory-made banjos with horrible mating problems in this area. First and most important, the inner seating surface of the tone ring must make intimate contact with the top of the wooden rim. You may inspect the top of your rim to make sure it is smooth and flat, and make sure that the outer skirt of the tone ring is not first bottoming-out against the rim, preventing a solid connection in the critical inner area. You may check this by slipping a piece of paper between the tone ring and rim. If it pulls out easily when the head is pushed down, you have poor contact and you'll have to scrape or machine down the wood around the outside of the rim until the tone ring seats properly.

Often people ask how tight a tone ring should fit upon the rim. I tell them that it should not rattle on the rim, but should be easy to pull off. The only trouble with this comment is that it can be true at one time of the year and not at another time of year. Humidity swells the wood rim and in the summer, the rim can grow by a surprising amount. Typically your tone ring will be very difficult to remove in the summer and just falls off the rim during dry spells in the winter. I have heard banjos with loose rings that sounded great and those with tight rings that sounded good. While this question is not as important as getting a good vertical fit, my personal preference is for a ring that slips off easily.

There may be questions you have about the holes in the tone rings. As I've come to understand it, these holes are for ventilation and don't serve much purpose other than to lighten up the ring a little. On a 40-hole arch top ring, the holes tend to sweeten up the tone somewhat compared to the heavier non-drilled arch top ring.

Cyclotronic and Timbre-Tronic Tone Rings

Nechville has been adding interest in the banjo world with their newer series of rolling rim designs. While the normal tone ring has intimate contact with the wood rim at the inner and usually outer parts of the tone ring, the cyclotronic rim makes contact with the tone ring only through a series of ball bearings. A flat surface plate or bearing race rests on the top center of the rim and the weight of the head's tension is transferred to it through up to 80 ball bearings that ride inside the cavity of the tone ring.

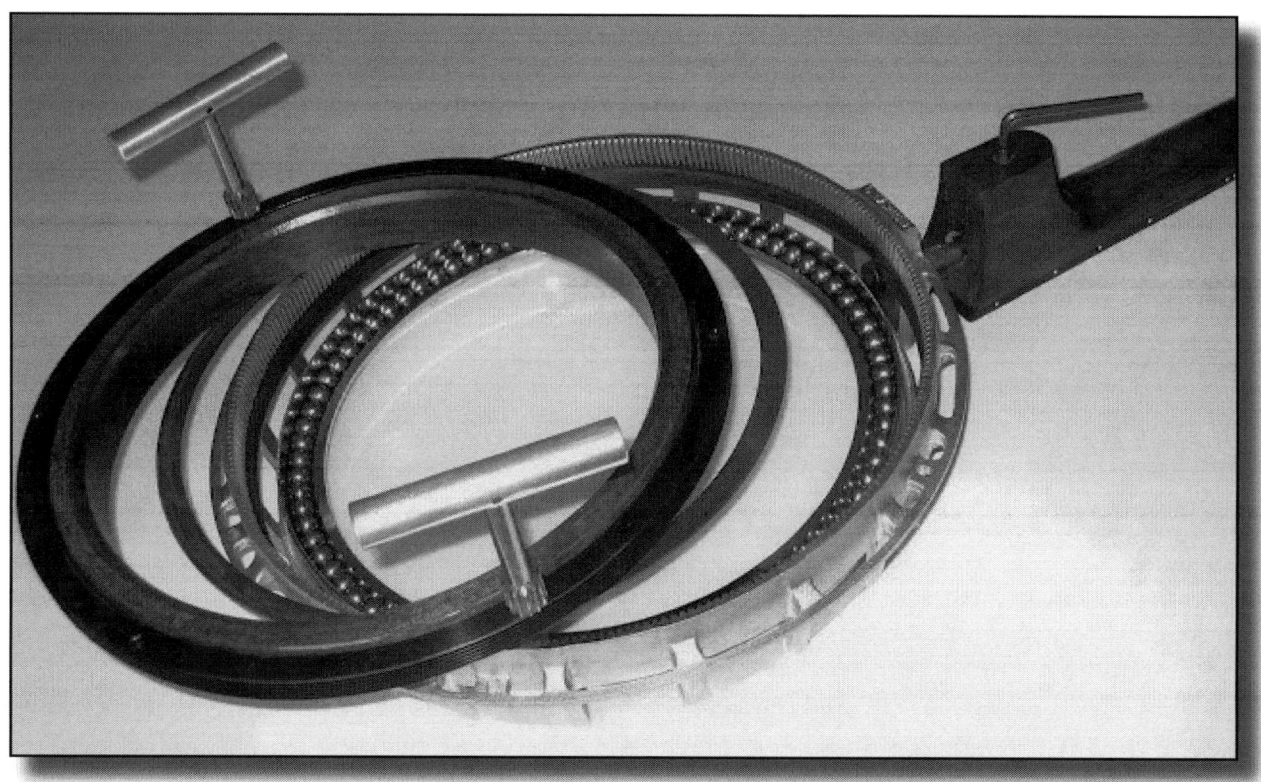

Inside Nechville's Cyclotronic pot assembly

Since this design does not depend on the normal tone ring to rim fit, it is possible to use tone rings without the side skirt, revealing the supporting ball bearings as viewed from the side of the banjo. The advent of no-skirt tone rings opened the door to exploration of many lighter weight options without a corresponding loss in volume or projection. Nechville now offers several models with Timbre-Tronic solid wood tone rings for a great woody resonant tone and significantly less weight.

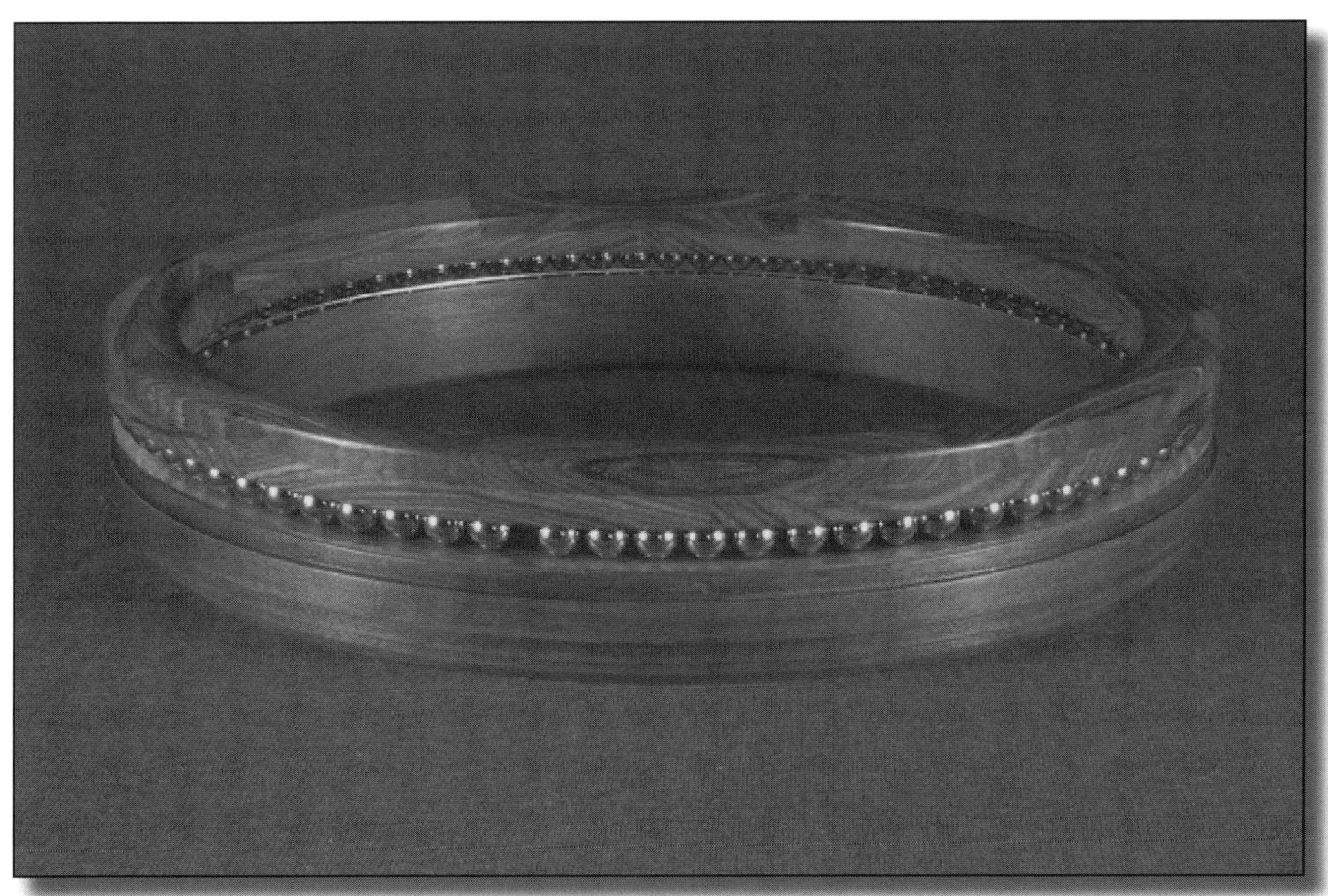
Timbr-Tronic Tone ring and rim

as installed in Heli-mount frame

Chapter Eight
Don't Crank Those Rods!

Many banjoists consider the metal reinforcing rods (coordinator rods) inside the banjo pot as just a handy way to adjust string action. However, it may surprise you to know that the main purpose for these rods is not for adjustment but for reinforcement. It is well-known among banjo builders that maladjusted coordinator rods is a common cause for poor-sounding banjos.

The coordinator rods are the main pieces of hardware that run through the center of a Mastertone-style banjo pot and serve to fasten the neck to the pot of the banjo. The other function of the rods is to give extra stability to the banjo pot. If there were not any rods, but rather just bolts to hold the neck on, the shape of the pot may eventually yield to the stress of the string tension and go out of round. This could cause unplayable action and/or uneven head tension leading to poor sound—among other mechanical problems. Since the rods span the diameter of the banjo, the stress of the neck connection (string tension) is spread to each side of the banjo pot. When adjusted properly, the rigidity of the metal rods maintains the cylindrical shape of the banjo pot.

It is a common practice among banjoists to adjust the coordinator rods in order to change the string action (the height of the strings from the fingerboard). While it is possible to alter the action via rod adjustment, most banjo experts advise against this practice.

The bottom rod extends through the rim opposite of the neck connection area. A bolt and washer is placed on each side of the wooden rim and snugged up to help stabilize the circular shape of the pot. If one were to loosen the inner bolt and tighten the outside bolt, the shape of the rim would actually distort enough to increase the effective back angle of the neck, hence lowering the action. Loosening the outer bolt and tightening the inner bolt would distort the pot the other direction, causing higher action.

It is best to secure the rods in their natural position while the string tension is relaxed, without adding stress to the rim either way. Any tightening of these bolts beyond their natural position creates stresses in the banjo rim that can detract from optimum sound.

Distortions from a misshapen rim can also affect the fit between the rim and tone ring. If a tone ring fits tight in some spots and loose in other spots, the natural resonance of the tone ring can be dampened, often leading to inferior sound. Excessive tightening of the coordinator rods or the outside bolt can cause physical damage as well, such as stripping out the entire neck connection stud, or causing the rim to delaminate.

The easiest way to alter the action of a banjo without using the coordinator rods for adjustment is to simply use a different height bridge. A small degree of action adjustment can be achieved by tightening and loosening the head, or possibly by an adjustment of the truss rod in the neck. But unless these alterations take you in the direction that you want to go, they are useless.

For example, if you tighten the truss rod to take all of the bow out of the neck in order to lower your action, you may be facing string rattling and buzzing. If you are looking for higher action, a higher bridge would often work well, but if you want to lower the action and can not use a lower bridge, you are stuck with the formidable task of re-cutting the heel of the neck to fit the pot at a more preferred angle. Unfortunately, this is an expensive and time-consuming job.

You will sometimes find banjos with a quick-fix shim wedged between the neck and rim. Since a rock-solid connection between a banjo neck and body is what gives the overall structure of the banjo rigidity, which is needed for good sustain and good volume, shims and/or gaps between the neck and body of a banjo are usually a bad idea—because they detract from a solid, stable connection. String energy and resulting volume and sustain are lost in such loose or spongy connections between the neck and body. But there are times when a well-made shim is the best option to get up and picking.

In the traditional banjo design, involving a direct connection between the neck and acoustic pot assembly, some distorting stresses to the rim are inevitable. The job of the coordinator rods should be to minimize the stresses rather than to add additional stresses by warping the rim and tone ring into providing unnatural string action.

The Flux Capacitor

It is appropriate here to add a note about my solution to coordinator rod and neck-fit problems. If a different neck angle is what you need, there is an interface part that can be added to your pot to make the neck adjustable. It does, however, require a new neck or at least a re-work to your neck's heel fit to employ this solution. The Flux Capacitor is a rigid metal part that connects to the pot via the coordinator rods, and the neck plugs on to the Flux, giving a wide range of neck angle adjustment to the neck. The Flux Capacitor also enables quick removal and transport of the body and neck separately. Contact Nechville to find a qualified retrofit advisor.

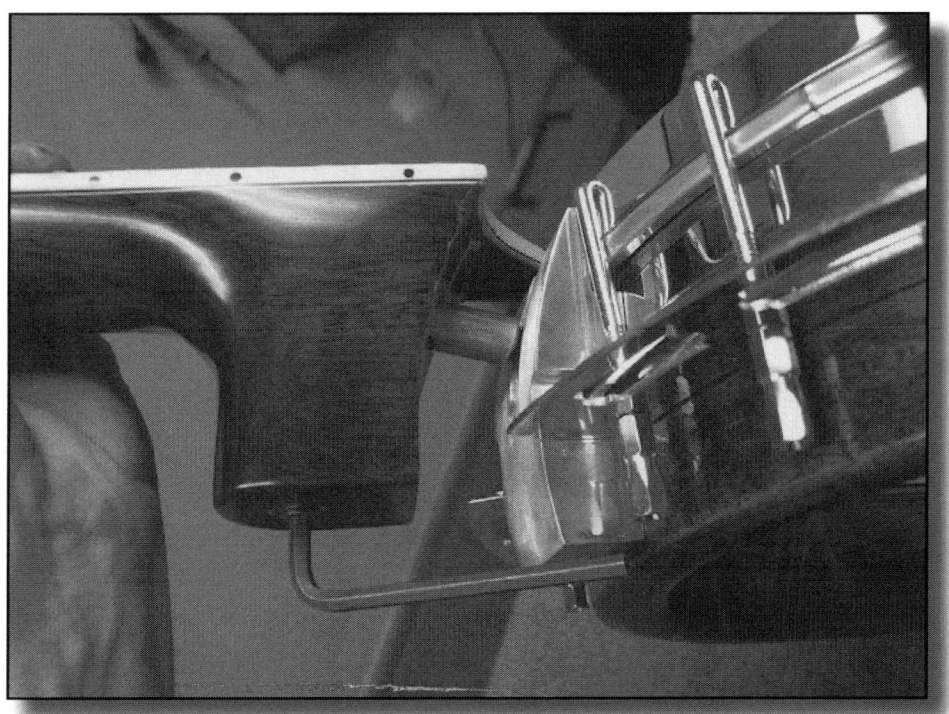

Chapter Nine
Fine Tuning Your Neck (and Other Intonation Secrets)

Nechville Musical Products offers repair service for all brands of banjos and other string instruments. A banjo player recently arrived with his new Gibson Scruggs Model for repair. Visually it was a beautiful piece of work, but he had been having difficulty keeping the instrument in tune—especially when he played up the neck. His problems, and our ensuing conversation regarding intonation, led us into several topics for discussion in this chapter.

Whenever I hear complaints about intonation problems up the neck, I start out by checking the position of the bridge, then inspecting the neck for the proper amount of bow, and then checking the nut for proper deepening of the string slots. With a good compensated bridge, you should be able to get any factory-built banjo to sing in tune everywhere on the neck. Let's look a little more specifically at each of these procedures.

Bridge Placement

To check the bridge's optimal position, start with the 1st string, and make a harmonic chime at the 19th fret. You make harmonic "chimes" by plucking a string while lightly touching the string precisely at the 12th or 19th fret. You are not actually touching the string against a fret, but simply dividing the string into equally vibrating nodes. These frets, along with others including the 7th and 5th, represent distances of 1/2, 1/3, or 1/4 of the overall string length. The chime at the 19th fret is the best one to use to find the most accurate bridge placement.

Compare the pitch of the 19th fret chime to the fully fretted note at the same fret. If the fretted note is sharp compared to the chimed note, move the bridge back toward the tailpiece. If the fretted note is flat, move the bridge forward. You'll notice changes with very little bridge movement.

Check each string and move the bridge accordingly, compromising between strings that do not agree. Use the 17th fret harmonic chime on the 5th string. If you have a straight bridge, your bridge will be angled after this process, giving more length to the 3rd, 4th, and 5th strings (because when the bridge is placed for proper intonation on the first string, it is noticeably off on the 3rd string). If you angle the bridge to correct for the 3rd string, the 4th and 5th strings will be off. Thicker, heavier strings require a little longer vibrating length to intonate properly. The wound 4th string on a banjo has a core wire that is thinner than the 3rd string, and therefore requires less scale length compensation. You may notice that lighter gauge strings require a bit less compensation because they do not vary much in thickness. I prefer medium light sets of 10, 12, 14, 22, 10 thousandths.

The best solution to the string gauge differential is to use a compensated bridge, giving a slightly longer vibrating length to the third string. Nechville makes the Enterprise Bridge. It has proper intonation for most 5-string banjo string sets and does not have to be angled to give correct vibrating length or intonation on every string.

Be sure that the bridge has not been tilted forward by the string tightening process. The bridge's feet should be flat on the head, and ideally the bridge should have some tilt backward toward the tailpiece. One other bit of bridge advice...Make sure that your bridge is not sagging in the middle. This causes difficulty in picking and increases the likelihood of the 3rd and 4th strings buzzing.

Neck Bow and Truss Rod Adjustment

Whenever you are evaluating a banjo for playability—or attempting to locate the source of string buzzes, you should check the amount of neck bow and adjust it if necessary. The easiest way to measure bow is to hold the 4th string down at the first fret and also hold it down at the 22nd fret. At the 7th fret there should be a space between the string and the top of the fret that is equal to the distance of about .015 "—a little thicker than a business card.

If the bow is greater, you will have problems, especially up the neck. If it is perfectly straight or back-bowed, you will also have problems, especially on the open strings.

Most good banjos have an adjustable truss rod accessible from the peghead end of the neck. Remove the truss rod cover and use a 1/4" socket driver (a screw driver with a 1/4" hex socket tip) to turn the nut. Some banjos might have a different size nut, but you can usually find a nut driver to fit. Some necks require an Allen wrench for adjustment. If you are removing back-bow or straightening the neck, you will turn the nut clockwise normally.

I often encourage the neck to move by putting some pressure on the neck in the direction I want it to go. Watch what you are doing by eyeing down the edge of the fingerboard. As you turn the rod's nut, you can see the neck straighten or bow. Watching as you go also tells you if you have one of those banjos with backwards threaded rods (in which case the result of clockwise turning is increased bow).

Leave the cover off and try the banjo to check for proper action and string clearance on every fret. Sometimes intonation problems will diminish with proper neck bow, because if the action is uniformly low, the string won't be stretching as far during fretting.

Fine-Tuning the Nut

You may have heard about compensating the nut to correct for poor intonation. Please do not try this on your banjo! It is only possible to do this on a new banjo, and whenever I have seen it done, it doesn't remedy intonation problems. What you can do, however, is to check the depth of the slots in the nut. They can be another source of trouble with intonation problems, especially in regard to the 2nd and 3rd strings.

To check the slots, hold the first string down between the 2nd and 3rd fret. Inspect the clearance between the first string and the first fret. There should be a tiny amount of clearance. You can tap on the string while holding it this way and actually hear the contact. Check the second string the same way, but take care to file the nut slot down to about .002" as checked with the above method. The higher the nut slot, the harder you have to push down the string to fret properly. Of course, it is critical that you not go too deep during this process, or you'll be faced with the repair that we'll discuss shortly. The 3rd string should have a bit more, about .003" clearance, and the 4th string should have about .004".

I use a 3-cornered triangle needle file. Alternately you can make a special tool yourself from a hacksaw blade. Pound the kerf out of the blade with a hammer on a flat hard surface. Then sand down or grind the sides of one end of the blade, being careful not to dull its cutting tips. The idea here is to thin the blade so you have a gradually widening taper to the blade. You can then cut various width slots just by using various parts of the blade.

Pull the string aside and use short strokes to deepen the rear of the slot more than the front edge (being careful not to scratch the peghead). Replace the string in the slot and test its depth again. If you discover that your slots are already too low or you accidentally went too far during this process, there is a quick fix that you can employ.

Clean out the slots and then use a fine file across the top of the nut until some bone shavings begin to fill up in the slots. Then, with a fine-tipped bottle of thin super-glue or "Hotstuff T," apply a tiny touch of glue to the low slot. You may want to use a dull knife edge to pack the glue and dust down into the slot for a solid repair. A shot with accelerator produces an instant cure, but beware that accelerator can ruin the finish on some banjos, especially those finished with lacquer. Finally, just re-slot the hole as described above and clean up with a single-edge razor blade. You'll be surprised how a properly slotted nut can improve the playability and intonation of your banjo!

Touch Up the Frets

Are your frets showing some wear? Do you have rough frets with visible sanding marks in them? If so, you deserve a smooth playing surface for smooth note bends and chokes. If your frets are severely gouged from playing a lot, they probably need replacing. But if they are just slightly worn, you can dress the frets yourself.

Remove the strings and put a couple layers of masking tape on the metal parts near the neck for protection. Also, protect the 5th string tuner from abrasion. Then take a black magic marker and darken the tops of each fret. Use a flat fine file—or better is a flat fine diamond stone—and gently slide the stone up and down the frets until you have removed the black from the tops of the highest frets. You'll be able to clearly see the black low spots that are the cause of trouble, so continue filing the frets higher up the neck until the fingerboard is level.

At this stage I usually round the tops of the frets with a fret file, which is available from Stewart-MacDonald. But there is another way to finish the frets that works nearly as well. Start with 320 or 400-grit sandpaper, going over the frets by hand until the file marks are gone. Then finish up with 1000 grit paper to put a nice shine on the frets. If you want to mask-off the wooden fingerboard surface, you can, but it's not necessary except on necks that display fine engraved details in the pearl. After sanding the fingerboard, the wood will be whitened and ugly looking, but you can rejuvenate it by using lemon oil and rubbing it up and down with the grain using a fine 3M pad or 0000 super-fine steel wool.

If you follow these set-up tips, you should be able to make any banjo sound and look its best—without taking it in to a professional repair shop!

Call Tom Nechville with questions...001 (952)-888-9710 or e-mail him...tom@nechville.com

Chapter Ten
Step-by-Step to Professional Banjo Set-Up

If you have read the rest of this book, you'll find this chapter a condensed review of material already covered. The following procedures can make a world of difference in how your banjo sounds. Following these steps will help revive your old banjo, and is a concise guide for achieving optimum sound on any banjo.

1. Neck Joint. Take off the resonator, and look inside. If you have a Mastertone style banjo (including most Bluegrass Banjos), there will be one or usually two coordinator rods inside. While holding the bottom rod itself from turning (by using a nail or small screwdriver stuck through the small hole in the coordinator rod), loosen the nuts on each side of the wooden rim opposite of where the neck attaches. Then make certain the neck is securely fastened to the rim via the coordinator rods, without shims or other obstacles in the way of a solid neck to rim fit. (If you have a visibly bad neck joint, you may want to scrape or sand down any high spots to get a better fit, but beware that this step is best left to a professional repair person.)

2. Secure coordinator rods. You should finger-tighten the loose nuts on the inside and outside of the rim. Give them a slight tightening with a wrench without stressing the rim and tone ring assembly. Hopefully you have improved the neck attachment and removed any stresses put into the rim and tone ring from improperly adjusted coordinator rods. It's a mistake to use the rods for more than a minute action adjustment. Any major change in playing action should be accomplished by changing bridges or re-cutting the heel to the appropriate angle.

3. Check Head Tension. If the head looks totally stretched out, or if there are any soft spots around the perimeter indicating that it's broken, it's time to change it. I recommend Remo Frosted heads. Even head tension is perhaps the most important step to professional sound. During re-assembly you may lubricate sticky or rusty nuts. If you have an ear for it, tune your head to a G♯ or 90 on a drum dial. Otherwise, just gradually tighten it a bit at a time until the head is VERY EVENLY tensioned and the tension hoop is level all the way around.

4. Adjust Tailpiece. Check that the tailpiece nut is not rattling. Start with the tailpiece straight (not pointed down). I like to tighten Presto style tailpieces until they touch the tension hoop and actually begin to teeter upwards slightly. Other set up pros tend to leave a presto quite high off the tension hoop. Tailpieces are often a cause of buzzing, and inefficiencies of sound transfer. You might consider replacing old tailpieces with an in-line tailpiece like a Price or Nechville. (Available from Nechville)

5. Truss Rod. Place the bridge in position (Fine tuning the bridge is explained in step 6) and determine if you need neck bow adjustment. Check the straightness of the neck by holding down a string at the first and last frets simultaneously. Then you can inspect the distance between the tops of the middle frets and the taught string. There should be a distance of only a millimeter or less, (.015 ") But make sure your neck is not too straight either. Normally a clockwise twist of the truss rod (accessible from the peghead of most banjos) will reduce the bow and straighten out a neck.

6. Intonate Bridge. Relocate the bridge for correct intonation. This is done by checking the harmonic at the 19th fret and comparing the note to the fretted note at the same fret. If the fretted note is sharp, move the bridge towards the tailpiece; if the fretted note is flat, move the bridge forward. Check the banjo's tuning and evaluate its playability.

7. Check Action. If your string height is around 1/8" away from the 12th fret, you are in luck! Try the banjo and see how it sounds. It's possible, however, that you have changed the neck angle and the resulting string action, so your banjo either has the strings laying on the frets or more likely, the action is way too high.

8. Install the correct bridge. It is best to have a little more height on the 3rd and 4th bridge slots for the best playability and the least string noise. Nechville makes the Enterprise Bridge in all sizes between 9/16 and 7/8".

The Enterprise is the only bridge I know that is weighed, radiused and compensated for optimal playability. If you still can't achieve low enough action with a low bridge, you may want to visit a luthier for increasing the neck's angle to accommodate a tall bridge, or consider a new neck with a Flux capacitor adjustable connection. It is best to use the tallest bridge possible for your banjo, but keep your bridge under 3 grams for normal sound.

9. Final adjustments. If your bow is correct, but still need to tweak the action, very slight coordinator rod adjustment can be made by first loosening the inner and outer nuts under the tailpiece. If the action needs raising, loosen the outside nut and tighten the inside nut. If the action needs to be lowered (which is usually the case), make sure the top nut by the head is tight, loosen the lower inside nut and tighten the outside nut under the tailpiece. Going too far with these nuts will warp the rim and cause damage—so be careful.

10. The last step is evaluating and plotting your next plan of attack. You may find that improvements were made but overshadowed by newfound fret buzzes after getting the action down. In this case, leveling the frets is in order. (A subject for another seminar)

Frequently it happens that clearing one problem exposes another. Listen carefully to each string both fretted and open. If you get fuzzy or dull sound on the open string, but not on the fretted string, your nut slots need attention, They may be too low, or simply worn out. You can revive the nut with a careful layer of super glue and bone dust in the slot and reshaping the slot. If you are happy, quit and enjoy playing the banjo. If you are a typical player, you'll continue the quest for the perfect sound. I hope someday soon I'll be building you a Nechville Helimount banjo.

Call Tom Nechville with questions... (952)-888-9710, or e-mail...tom@nechville.com.

Chapter Eleven
How to Play the Banjo

Having a banjo that sounds great is only the starting point. Once your instrument is sounding its best, I want to hear it. I want to turn on the radio or TV and hear you playing the banjo. I want the sound of the banjo to find a place in everyday music.

How can we play the banjo so that this dream can happen? We need you to keep playing the things that you can do best. Take every opportunity to add your own signature to your music. Play proudly. You don't have to invent a whole new style of picking, but if your tastes pull you toward the inventive, creative side, let it be heard.

Play for your neighbors; teach a kid how to play something. Show people how fun it is to play and entertain with the banjo. Try to find other musicians who bring you new musical perspectives. Learn from them and show them what you know.

If you are truly a beginner, or are inspired by the idea of playing, and really want to know where and how to start, I'll tell you. It's really easy to tell, but hard to execute. Obviously practice is the key, and lots of it, but you need to know what to practice and when to go on to the next thing. I'd say most people make the mistake of trying too much at first, and moving ahead before they learn the basics. I can't say much about 4-string techniques, and clawhammer styles of 5-string, but if you are interested in 3 finger picking style of 5-string banjo, let me give you my formula for success.

Start with chords. Learn the 3 common major shapes for the left hand, and start memorizing all the G's C's and D's in different places. Get fast at changing chords to simple 3 chord songs without loosing the beat of the music. Use recorded music when possible, or have a partner provide rhythm while you simply strum on the back beat. Think of "boom-chick boom-chick" and you strum on the "chick."

Try to understand what notes of the scale make up major chords and minor chords. Eventually you will add to your knowledge of theory, but once you can change chords in time and begin knowing a few different places to make the same chord, it is time to employ some simple picking patterns to use along with the chord changes. You don't necessarily need picks right away, but put them on when you are ready. You'll need them when it's time to go out and jam. When the picks go on, spend lots of time with a tiny pliers and make them feel comfortable. Experiment with positioning your picking hand and finger tips to contact the string squarely and try to bend the picks to enhance the perpendicularity of a clearly picked note.

The first pattern defines the "boom-chick" and I call it a "pinch" pattern. The thumb strikes down on a middle string for the "boom" and you pinch the 1st, 2nd and 5th strings together for the "chick." Patterns repeat with the right hand over and over, and thousands of reps are needed to get smooth and automatic. You'll play all the songs you know with the pinch pattern or strums, making sure that you are always singing along in your head, or out loud if you can. When you are ready, you can add more complicated right hand patterns, or rolls, and just plug them in to your songs. Start with a 4 note Square roll, Make it smooth and quick before worrying about the next one. You'll soon add the slide to that square roll, making the famous "Cripple Creek" roll. Do it 10,000 times. When you have mastered everything including the square roll with slide, you already have a fairly good selection of tools in your musical toolkit. The idea is to gradually add building blocks such as Forward rolls, Reverse rolls, Backward rolls, and Alternating finger or thumb rolls, Then start mastering a few left hand techniques like slides, pull-offs, hammer-ons, and chokes. It's is easy to tell someone how to play, but actually "getting it" is a matter of hard work, building muscle memory and stamina, callouses, and quickness.

Your progression as a player will be influenced by a number of factors, and I would put them in the following order of importance.

1. How much time you practice
2. Confidence in knowing your practice will pay off
3. Who you have around encouraging your practice
4. Your patience and stamina for long periods of practice
5. Your good practice partners
6. Finding success and having fun during practice
7. Your talent for musical sounding practice
8. How you discipline your practice
9. Your comfortable practice space
10. Your knowledge of music in general or knowing another instrument

We at Nechville Musical Products are interested in what you are up to in the banjo world. Drop me a note and pass along your own favorite banjo set-up tips, product information, or commentaries for publication in our quarterly newsletter, Nechville News (also available online).

The banjo is alive and growing because of you and people like you. Thanks for your enthusiasm and love for this instrument. Keep in Touch!
tom@nechville.com

Emily Robison (Dixie Chicks) playing her "Gus" custom Classic

Appendix
Notes from the Author

As a lifelong banjo player, performer, and luthier, my dream has been a "maintenance-free" instrument with fewer of the problems inherent in conventional banjos. The prerequisite, however, is clean, pure musical tone and easy playability. The quest goes on day by day in the Banjo Lab at NMP, but I can honestly say that this goal has been 99 % realized with Nechville Helimount banjos.

The Heli-Mount two-piece frame idea originated as a method for producing perfectly even head tensioning. Rather than having 24 points of tension around the perimeter of the banjo head that can be unevenly tensioned, the Helimount banjo has only one continuous threaded connection which virtually screws together like the cap on a jar. The added benefits of an independently adjustable neck and a "free floating" tone ring came as logical extensions of the basic Heli- Mount mechanism.

Soon after the Heli-Mount was born, We devised an equally innovative neck design. The NUVO neck was designed and also patented. In the late 1980s. My designs were ready to meet the critical review of the pro pickers in Nashville.

From 1990 to the present I have been busy expanding Helimount production capabilities, and developing a whole line of new electric banjos that have been seen among the world's musical superstars. I'm always looking toward the future with players' success in mind. Please let me know if you'd like help realizing some of your banjo dreams.

I want to give special thanks to some inspiring and helpful friends and travel companions, Val Johnson, Tedd Williams, Al Price and Rick Sampson, My lovely Wife Jane Nechville, My editor and fun sister Jamie Peterson, my great dealers like Turtle Hill, my banjo-playing heros, Bela Fleck, Noam Pickelney, and Alison Brown, for not only inspiring me through their music, but for challenging me into new designs and on to new frontiers in banjo sounds. Many thanks to all my customers who have believed in a better idea, and had the courage and spirit to invest in something new even during hard economic times. Thanks to Dave Hill, office manager, Dan Schultz the shop manager, Bruce Davison the facilities manager, Wayne Sagmoen head builder, and Jeremiah Lindstrom for doing it all, And everyone else who has played a role in the BANJO REVOLUTION!

— Tom Nechville

Three Amigos L to R Lluis Gomez-Spain, Leon Hunt-England, Tim Carter-USA

Tom and Charmin in the Nechville showroom

About the Author

Tom Nechville, inventor, designer, and builder of the revolutionary Heli-Mount banjo, ENTERPRISE Bridge, Meteor Electric Banjos, the Banjovie mini banjo, Flex-Tone banjos and more, ... began playing the 5-string when he was in his early teens. Tom is president of Nechville Musical Products, and is also a professional banjoist, having been part of the Midwest bluegrass bands Backroads Junction, Strawberry Jam, Middle Spunk Creek Boys, and Tamarac. He is a professional member of the American Society of Independent Luthiers, International Bluegrass Music Association, Minnesota Bluegrass and Old Time Music Association, and the National Association of Music Merchants. In 1991, and in 2011 Tom received patents on his Heli-Mount banjo designs and technology, and has spent over a quarter century designing and building custom instruments for serious banjoists worldwide.

Tom travels extensively and holds the record for the most travel with the fewest hotel bills. He has survived accidental dosage of windshield washer fluid after ingesting a bag of red-hot Cheetos during a solo shot to Nashville one late night in the 1990's. Another night in the new millennium, after having unknowingly stopped to rest along the barbed wire outside the prison of the murder capital, Flint Michigan, he was greeted by an officer asking for I.D. His wallet being in his pants at home didn't help sell the story of him being an international banjo executive en route to Canada and after an embarrassing interrogation with reinforcements at hand, Nechville put on a small concert for the troopers to prove his identity. More favorite stories from the travels of Nechville can be found on line at www.nechville.com/ blog.

Tom resides in Bloomington, Minnesota, with his wife Jane. They travel the world attending music events and spreading the joy of the BANJO REVOLUTION. Look for them at the next Bluegrass festival you attend.

Tom and Norway's Terje Kinn during a workshop in Oslo

Nech-tology 101
A Glossary of Nechville Terms

Atlas Banjo — This banjo is a design by Tom Nechville and Wayne Sagmoen, an expert in open back banjo design. The pot (banjo body) is similar to that of an Ashborn banjo from the 1860's. It has a wooden flange which reduces the number of metal parts on the instrument, and makes it more comfortable to play. The adjustable, detachable neck, which is a Nechville patented design, are innovative features which are found on all Nechville models.

Banjovia — Name changed to Nechville News Quarterly Newsletter. Keep up with news from the front lines of banjo design plus set-up and player information to keep you sounding your best.

Capobility — Nechville's patented straight neck with full length 5th string, built-in main rolling capo with sliding 5th string peg for quick key changes without re-tuning. There are 5 extra notes to use on the 5th string due to the extra width down to the nut.

Cascade Inlay — Designed by Larry Breelove of Breedlove guitars, and became a signature Nechville look as featured on the popular Nextar model.

Comfort Bevel Armrest — Due to its ergonomic design, Nechville's exotic wood armrest increases your comfort through extended periods of play without stress or fatigue on your right arm.

Cosmos Meteor — A synth ready polyphonic electric banjo without a conventional head, but able to instantly trigger any sound through a guitar synthesizer or Midi patch.

Cyclotronic Tone Ring — Designed specifically for **Nechville's Heli-mount** banjos. The helical turning motion that is required to tighten a Heli-mount head gives the rim a tendency to turn. The mechanism Nechville uses for eliminating turning friction and for mounting of the tone ring is called the Cyclotronic System. If you imagine what I've heard of called a "cyclotron," with electrons chasing around a big circle and smashing into each other, you might see where I got the name for this series of ball bearings or "tone Spheres" that roll around inside the tone ring and above the rim. There is a metal cap on wooden rims to prevent the balls from digging into the rim. This design allows for easy tightening of the Helimount's head while the tone ring mounts in a completely non-dampened way.

The Enterprise Bridge — Nechville's own precision-weighed, measured, compensated 5-string banjo bridge. Made from select maple and ebony.

Flux Capacitor — Nechville's flexible mounting port between a modern Nechville neck and a historic banjo pot is called the **Flux Capacitor**. The **Flux Capacitor** is firmly connected to the traditional pot via the existing coordinator rods and enables the neck to be locked in at various angles to control string height. The new neck is simply plugged on and locked to create a **"Flex-tone"** hybrid banjo.

Heli-mount Banjo — The alternate style of head tension, introduced to the world of bluegrass during the decade of the 1990s, is known as helical head mounting. Nechville, the inventor and patent holder of helical head mounting, continues to make the new design accessible to more players each year. Differing dramatically from the traditional design, the drum body or "pot" comprised of the tone ring and rim is mounted concentrically into a metal frame called a Heli-Mount, which is fastened to the neck. There is a singular screw thread around the inside perimeter of the Heli-mount frame that acts like the threaded ridges around the lip of a jar. A threaded mating retaining ring is turned into the back of the frame, securing and tightening the tone ring, or rim body against the head. Nechville has been producing Helimount banjos continually since their invention in 1986.

Meteor Banjos — Electric players can choose from various options including Midi-Synth, 6 string, onboard effects, and more. Without the fear of feedback this instrument is equipped with an active EMG magnetic pickup as well as a piezo pickup which brings out a natural, high-quality banjo sound. Virtuoso banjoist Bela Fleck had an influence in this instrument's development working with designer Tom Nechville. You'll see Meteors on the road with top groups like The Flecktones, Bruce Springsteen, Zac Brown, and Keith Urban band.

Nuvo — Nechville's Straight necked banjo, not profiled for the 5th string, giving additional playability to the 5th string, and instant "Capo-bility" with its built in capo system.

Phantom — Nechville's popular banjo featuring a tunneled, or hidden 5th string so that the 5th string's tuner can be placed up and away from the side of the banjo neck, so it does not get in the way of left hand fingering.

Timbre-Tronic Tone ring — A no-skirt wooden tone ring made of solid Cocobolo segments mounted on a series of ball bearings, similar to the Cyclotronic, but lighter in weight and offers a punchy, warm tone.

Turbo Module — The Turbo Module is an add-on that will replace the head, tone ring, and rim of any Heli-mount Nechville acoustic banjo, transforming into one of Nechville's Meteor Electric Banjos.

Universal Meteor — A meteor with built in polyphonic pickups and preamp for direct triggering of synthesizers and midi sounds.

Visit Our Website: www.nechville.com
001 (952) 888-9710
e-mail: tom@nechville.com
Find Tom Nechville or Nechville banjos on Facebook

Notes

Notes